D1553627

Charles Knevitt is architecture correspondent of *The Times*. Born in America in 1952, of British parents, he was educated at Stonyhurst and the University of Manchester School of Architecture, editor of *What's new in Building*, 1978–80, architecture correspondent of the *Sunday Telegraph*, 1980–84, and architecture/planning consultant to *Thames News*, 1983–86. He received the International Building Press Architectural Journalist of the Year Award in 1984.

His previous books are *Manikata: The Making of a Church*, 1980; *Connections: The Architecture of Richard England 1964–84*, 1984; *Space on Earth: Architecture – People and Buildings*, 1985, a companion to the six-part Anglia Television series for Channel Four; and *Monstrous Carbuncles: A Cartoon Guide to Architecture*, editor, 1985. He is co-author, with Nick Wates, of *Community Architecture: How people are shaping their own Environment*, published by Penguin Books in 1987.

Louis Hellman is an architect, writer and illustrator, and has been the regular cartoonist on *The Architects' Journal* since 1967. Born in London in 1936, he read architecture at University College London, and has contributed numerous articles to professional journals such as *Building Design, Built Environment, RIBA Journal*, as well as the *AJ*. In 1974 he made an animated cartoon history of modern architecture, 'Boom', for BBC Television. His work has been exhibited at the Architectural Association and the London Building Centre, including his famous 'Archi-Têtes' caricatures.

He has published two collected books of cartoons, *A is for Architect*, 1975; and *All Hellman Breaks Loose*, 1980. *Architecture for Beginners*, a cartoon history of architecture, was recently published by Allen & Unwin.

Architecture is very much like the oldest profession in the world:
it has only one aim, and that is to please for a fee.
Philip Johnson

A bicycle shed is a building; Lincoln Cathedral is a piece of architecture. Nearly
everything that encloses space on a scale sufficient for a human being to move
in is a building; the term architecture applies only to buildings designed with a
view to aesthetic appeal.
Sir Nikolaus Pevsner

The desire to bomb a virgin building is terrific.
Commander Henry Urban Jnr

Perspectives

An Anthology of 1001 Architectural Quotations

Edited by Charles Knevitt

Illustrated by Louis Hellman

With a Foreword by Sir Hugh Casson

Lund Humphries · London
in association with

Bovis   1837 P&O 1987

First published 1986

Published in association with Bovis
(a member of the P&O Group)
by Lund Humphries Publishers Ltd
124 Wigmore Street, London W1
Distributed to the book trade by
SPA Books Ltd
PO Box 47, Stevenage, Herts SG2 8UH

ISBN 0 85331 511 6

Designed by Alan Bartram
Typeset by TNR Productions Ltd, London
Printed in Great Britain by
Camelot Press, Southampton

Acknowledgements
The editor would like to thank all those who submitted
suggestions for inclusion, especially Dr John Parker of
Greater London Consultants, A Roderick Males, Walter
Ritchie, Richard England, Louis Hellman, Sam Webb
and Professor Sir George Grenfell-Baines. Other
contributors were: Manfred Berlowitz, J Dunthorne,
Christopher Teague, Ken Dixon, John R Wharton,
Geraint John, R M Renshaw, Peter J Hawker, Bob
Smyth, Perry Sennitt, Dick Gardner, Christopher J
Willis, James D Newcombe, Sydney Downs, Professor
Christopher Riley, Thomas A Baruffati, Rod Hackney,
Michael Adams, A Jarvis, Peter Beldham and John
Dunthorne. He would also like to thank the following
for their help in various ways: Stephen J Gash of Bovis;
Nancy Price, formerly of Bovis; the editors of *Building*
and *Building Design*; John Taylor, Charlotte Burri and
Eveline van Rooy of Lund Humphries Publishers; Sara
Drake of A D Peters & Co; Anne Cowlin for her
secretarial assistance; and Nancy Young for compiling
the indexes.

Contents

Foreword

'Mots justes' are elusive quarry. They require a sharp eye to spot and a sharper nose to detect their flavour and then to extract the gold and the sparkle from the prosy, the sententious or the smarty-pants. The author of this collection is blessed with such an eye and nose. He has clearly enjoyed using them and, even more importantly, he conveys that enjoyment to us.

Here are around a thousand sayings made about the single subject of architecture. The restriction of subject adds extra flavour to the snap crackle pop of their variety and interest. Epigrams as polished as bicycle bells, aphorisms (pompous or perceptive), proverbs (heavy with the obvious), wise-cracks concealing a large truth in a tiny joke which explodes at once or operates on a slow fuse. Like all the best anthologies, this is a personal selection – and that's its fun and interest for the reader who may find and enjoy, in totting up the scores, some surprises among those old professionals.

Shakespeare, the Bible and Anon, Ruskin, Frank Lloyd Wright, Le Corbusier and the Prince of Wales you would expect – but lively strangers include Pasternak and Vogue, Rodin and Billy Rose, Orwell and Seifert, Spike Milligan and John Milton! Philip Johnson does better than Samuel, but Philip Larkin, Kenneth Clark and the *Architectural Review* only just squeeze in. (Current taste in potted wisdom is obviously as volatile as it is in architecture itself and is equally entertaining to pursue and pin down.)

Understandably, it is an English collection. There is little from Europe or the Orient and nothing from Africa. But good anthologists are not expected to be impartial and rightly wander in fields of their own choice, picking only the flowers that attract them. In making this collection Charles Knevitt takes us with him and the journey is throughout a delight.

Sir Hugh Casson

For Richard and Myriam

Preface

Authors can spend a professional lifetime compiling an anthology and still feel that their *opus* is incomplete. No matter how diligent they are new sources will always come to light and obvious omissions be brought to their attention. *Perspectives* is the result of reading – and dipping into – hundreds of sources over 15 years. It is not intended to be comprehensive – but it is a start. While books of proverbs, aphorisms and after-dinner speeches, and anthologies on music, literature and travel abound, this is the first time, to my knowledge, that a collection on architecture has been published.

As Sir Hugh Casson writes in his Foreword, the 1001 quotations are a personal choice. There is a conscious bias towards contemporary examples and those which seem to be particularly relevant: quotations which reflect the renewed interest in the art of architecture, the pitfalls of practice, and the role – not always creative – of critics. Places, both home and abroad, feature strongly. Builders and the process of building make an appearance. Many individual works of architecture are discussed; what was said about the Crystal Palace, St Pancras Station and Tower Bridge at the time they were opened go to prove that present-day controversy over the new Lloyd's headquarters and the National Gallery extension have their precedents. If anything, critics today are much kinder to their prey.

This collection is aimed, primarily, at the casual reader who will browse through it as a welcome distraction to some particularly troublesome detail on the drawing board, tedious meeting with a committee or client, or argument over a hopelessly optimistic bill of quantities. For the more serious writer or historian it combines many popular references with those which are elusive and obscure; these may be divined from the indexes on authors and subjects at the back. Enjoyment has been the principal criterion for selection.

To quote Dr John Parker's definition of a quotation, it is 'something that someone has said at sometime that seemed quite sensible'. Examples of impenetrable prose, so common among architectural writers, have been omitted on the grounds of their insensibility. No doubt the following quotation by the Italian critic Manfredo Tafuri, taken from his *Theories and History of Architecture*, sounds marvellous in his native tongue, but it has no value (apart from immediate amusement value) elsewhere in this book:

'Somehow we could consider Levi-Strauss the Parmenides of this neo-Eleatic flavoured (*malgré soi*) philosophy: structure and order against disorder in history, the permanence of Being against the phenomenology of Becoming, the stability of the common mechanisms to which man is reduced against Sartrian dialectical reason (but one is already beginning to see the first skirmishes of the neo-Zenoni demolishing paradoxes).'

Quite!

The temptation to rely more heavily on the Bible, Shakespeare, Dickens or Johnson (Samuel, not Philip) has been resisted. Louis Hellman, apart from his cartoons, is prominent as architecture's own Edward Lear; his limericks, published here for the first time, were a joy to discover. But for me, it was Sir John Betjeman who first brought architecture alive with his incisive and unpatronising prose, his mockery of professional foibles and his sending up of all that smacked of false progress or the misrepresentation of the ephemeral as substantial. Only Sir Osbert Lancaster, his friend and colleague from the *Architectural Review* in the days before the Second World War, comes close.

Although this anthology is more of a pot-pourri of quotations than a textbook, which is how Betjeman described his *Ghastly Good Taste*, written in 1933, it is with his *raison d'être* for that book that I want to sign off. His sentiments are not entirely my own, but then that has never been the best method of selecting material for publication. Merely, his verve and style deserve emulation by all those who would wish to be remembered, if for no other contribution to this world, than for their 'quotable quotes':

'There is little reason for my continuing the rest of the book beyond pleasing my publisher, and indulging my own pleasure in writing and gaining that money which I cannot come by honestly. Architecture suffers from never being dealt with in pamphlets – always in books. A page of illustrations of good and bad buildings will do more than a chapter of text. Here is another textbook, an opportunity for the thousands of "art critics", of whom I am unwillingly one, to air their pedantry and express their annoyance, an opportunity for aesthetic snobs to contest yet another theory; but if one copy of this book goes to every Institute for the Training of Museum Officials, for Preserving the Countryside, for Affiliating Incorporated Painter-Stainers, for Painting and Staining Incorporated Institutes, and to every other body for the official expression of aesthetic self-consciousness, I shall have made enough money to get myself up in an arty manner, and so qualify for a lectureship at some Ruskin School of Art, there to pronounce dicta admired and uncriticised for the rest of my life – an acknowledged "expert" whose opinion will be valuable to Americans.'

Charles Knevitt
Teddington, Middlesex
October 1986

Architecture is . . .

¶1

Architecture is very much like the oldest profession in the world. It has only one aim, and that is to please for a fee.

Philip Johnson (1984)

¶2

A bicycle shed is a building; Lincoln Cathedral is a piece of architecture. Nearly everything that encloses space on a scale sufficient for a human being to move in is a building; the term architecture applies only to buildings designed with a view to aesthetic appeal.

Sir Nikolaus Pevsner *opening lines of 'An Outline of European Architecture' (1943)*

¶3

Architecture is music in space, as it were a frozen music.

Friedrich Von Schelling *'Philosophie der Kunst'*

¶4

I call architecture 'petrified music'. Really there is something in this; the tone of mind produced by architecture approaches the effect of music.

Johann Wolfgang von Goethe *quoted in Johann Peter Eckermann's 'Conversations with Goethe' (23 March 1829)*

¶5

The sight of such a monument is like a continuous and stationary music.

Madame de Staël *'Corinne' Bk iv, ch 3*

¶6

Good architecture is like a piece of beautifully composed music crystallized in space that elevates our spirits beyond the limitation of time.

Tao Ho *quoted in 'Contemporary Architecture' (1980)*

¶7

Three things are to be looked to in a building; that it stand on the right spot; that it be securely founded; that it be successfully executed.

Johann Wolfgang von Goethe *'Elective Affinities'*

¶8

The moulding and altering to human needs of the very face of the earth itself.

William Morris

¶9

The history of architecture is the history of the world.

Augustus W N Pugin (1843)

¶10

The history of civilisation . . . leaves in architecture its truest, because its most unconscious, record.

Geoffrey Scott

¶11

Living on borrowed light.

Louis Hellman

¶12

In the same way that music requires notion, an idea that unifies tones, pauses and rhythms, architecture requires an idea that structures form, space and rhythm as a unity.

Henning Larsen

¶13

If there are many equally valid technical solutions to a problem, the one which offers the user a message of beauty and emotion, that one is architecture.

Luis Barragán

¶14

Architecture is the transformation of mental substance into material dimensions.

Justus Dahinden

¶15

Architectural space can only be defined as the collision of geometric and physiological space.

Raimund Abraham

¶16
Every act of construction is an act of defiance to nature.
   Emilio Ambasz

¶17
Architecture which started as a path to enlightenment, has now ended up as a
route to speculation.
   Richard England

¶18
Architecture is the manifestation of the dreams we desire.
   Richard England

¶19
The masterly, correct and magnificent play of masses brought together in light.
   Le Corbusier

¶20
Architecture is a machine for the production of meaning.
   Arata Isozaki *quoted in 'Contemporary Architects' (1980)*

¶21
Less is more.
   Ludwig Mies van der Rohe (c.1923)

¶22
Less is less.
   Ken Dixon *in a dissertation, School of Architecture, Cape Town (1955)*

¶23
Less is a bore.
   Robert Venturi *'Complexity and Contradiction in Architecture' (1966)*

¶24
Less is only more where more is no good.
   Frank Lloyd Wright

¶25
Architecture is inhabited sculpture.
   Constantin Brancusi *quoted in Igor Stravinsky's 'Themes and Episodes' (1966)*

¶26
Architecture is pre-eminently the art of significant forms in space – that is, forms
significant of their functions.
   Claude Bragdon *'Wake Up and Dream', in 'Outlook' (27 May 1931)*

¶27
Architecture has been defined as 'building plus delight'.
   Sir Ove Arup *quoted in 'The Architects' Journal' (1966)*

¶28

All architecture is great architecture after sunset.
G K Chesterton

¶29

Architecture is fantasy made of precisions.
Gio Ponti

¶30

An architecture of evolution not revolution.
Richard England

¶31

The problem with modern architecture is that it tried to find a universal solution to what was never a universal problem.
Richard England

¶32

Architecture is a chain whose links are space and time.
Richard England

¶33

When all is said and done there remains the building.
Richard England

¶34

Creativity in architecture is the joining of head and heart in a joyous response to life.
Richard England

¶35

An architect should mix the tenses of the site.
Richard England

¶36

Every architect is on every other architect's menu.
Richard England

¶37

Architects should strive to create a work of architecture where the floor is the earth, the walls are the wind and the ceiling is the sky.
Richard England

¶38

Tradition is the alphabet
Form is the language
Architecture is the poem.
Richard England

¶39

Ah, to build, to build!
That is the noblest art of all the arts.
Painting and sculpture are but images,
Are merely shadows cast by outward things
On stone or canvas, having in themselves
No separate existence. Architecture,
Existing in itself, and not in seeming
A something it is not, surpasses them
As substance shadow.

Henry Wadsworth Longfellow 'Michael Angelo' Pt 1, sec 2, l 54

¶40

The reason for architecture is to encourage people . . . to behave, mentally and physically, in ways they had previously thought impossible.

Cedric Price

¶41

Architecture is more than a reflective act of civilisation. It is a regenerative force.

Colin Naylor quoted in 'Contemporary Architects' (1980)

¶42

Architecture provokes spiritual reactions in man . . . the mission of architects is to make these explicit.

Adolf Loos

¶43

Architecture is too important to be left to architects alone. Like a crime, it is a problem for society as a whole.

Berthold Lubetkin RIBA President's invitation lecture (1985)

¶44

[Today's] buildings are not architecture, but packaging glued together with epoxy or neoprene . . . It is all a technological funfair of the shifty age of make-believe, high turnover, low-profile, cover operations and massage parlours. Indeed, as could be expected, our art reflects vividly a demented society that has had its day.

Berthold Lubetkin RIBA President's invitation lecture (1985)

¶45

In architecture the pride of man, his triumph over gravitation, his will to power, assume a visible form. Architecture is a sort of oratory of power by means of forms.

Friedrich Nietzsche 'Skirmishes in a War with the Age', 'Twilight of the Idols' (1888)
Translation by Antony M Ludovici

¶46

[He] admitted with 'resignation and even despair, that the finest achievements of modern architecture do not compete with the finest achievements of the past, which display a richness, plentitude, and splendour in dramatic contrast to the drabness and chaos of our own cities and buildings'.

Sir Herbert Read

¶47.

Architecture means the thoughtful housing of the human spirit in the physical world.

William O Meyer *quoted in 'Contemporary Architects' (1980)*

¶48

Architecture has little or nothing to do with the invention of interesting forms or of personal inclinations. True architecture is always objective and is the expression of the inner structure of our time from which it stems.

Ludwig Mies van der Rohe *quoted in 'Mies van der Rohe' by Werner Blaser (1965)*

¶49

Architecture is the will of an epoch translated into space.

Ludwig Mies van der Rohe *quoted in 'New York Herald Tribune' obituary (1969)*

¶50

What has happened to British architecture since the second world war that the only passers-by who can contemplate it without pain are those equipped with a white stick and a dog?

Bernard Levin *article in 'The Times' (1983)*

¶51

Architecture is the art of resolving our needs for physical shelter harmoniously with the environment, while responding to visual aspirations, thus contributing to our cultural heritage.

Gustavo de Roza *quoted in 'Contemporary Architects' (1980)*

¶52

An art for all to learn because all are concerned with it.

John Ruskin

¶53

Architecture is the work of nations.

John Ruskin *'True and Beautiful: Sculpture'*

¶54

Architecture is the total of man's manmade physical surroundings. The only thing I leave out is nature. You might say it is manmade nature. It is the total of everything we have around us . . . It is man's total physical surroundings, outdoors and indoors.

Eero Saarinen *quoted in 'Time' (1956)*

¶55

Architecture has its political use.
   Sir Christopher Wren

¶56

... after all, architecture is an art and from time immemorial it has been
regarded as one of the greatest. Beautiful buildings, the Parthenon, for instance,
Chartres, or St Paul's have moved men more profoundly than any but the very
greatest masterpieces of painting and sculpture: but who is going to be moved,
except by resentment, by buildings such as Herr Mendelsohn produces or M Le
Corbusier in France, or by buildings of steel and brick that purport to be made of
concrete, buildings cased in steel and glass, buildings that appear to follow no
principle but that of contradicting everything that has ever been done before? I
suggest that our modernists are wrong in principle.
   Sir Reginald Blomfield (1932)

¶57

Architecture is the frame of human existence. Architecture is the only record you
can read now of those civilisations which have passed into the distance.
   Frank Lloyd Wright *quoted in 'The Sunday Times' (1957)*

¶58

Architecture is the art of creating a space.
   Yoshinobu Ashihara *quoted in 'Contemporary Architects' (1980)*

¶59

Architecture is not the answer to the pragmatic needs of man, but the answer to
his passions and imagination.
   Emilio Ambasz

¶60

The problem of architecture as I see it is the problem of all art – the elimination
of the human element from the consideration of form.
   Evelyn Waugh's *character Professor-Architect Otto Friedrich Silenus quoted in 'Decline
   and Fall'*

¶61

Architecture is what you do to a building when you look at it.
   Walt Whitman

¶62

In Architecture as in all other Operative Arts, the end must direct the Operation.
The end is to build well. Well-building hath three Conditions: Commodity,
Firmness, and Delight.
   Sir Henry Wotton *'Elements of Architecture' (1624)*

¶63

Architecture can never be produced by men that have lost the power to wonder.
   Ralph Tubbs *'The Englishman Builds' (1945)*

¶64

Architecture is not sinks and fitted furniture. When passion so fires the use of inert materials that they touch our deepest feelings, that is architecture.

Ralph Tubbs *'The Englishman Builds' (1945)*

¶65

Architecture is to masonry what poetry is to literature.

Anon

¶66

[Architecture] is an art purely of invention – and invention is the most painful and most difficult exercise of the human mind.

Sir John Soane

¶67

Ninety-nine per cent of modern architecture [is] boring, banal, and barren, and usually disruptive and unharmonious when placed in older cities.

James Stirling *speaking at Yale University (1974)*

¶68

A building is a string of events belonging together.

Chris Fawcett *quoted in 'Contemporary Architects' (1980)*

¶69

Architecture should inspire people. I think it was Einstein who said of Le Corbusier's work that it was a kind of vision that made it easy to do good and difficult to do evil. I think that is exactly what architects have to do.

Bruce Graham (1984)

¶70

A particle is snatched from space, rhythmically modulated by membranes dividing it from surrounding chaos; that is Architecture.

Ernö Goldfinger *quoted in 'Contemporary Architects' (1980)*

¶71

Architecture cannot lie, and buildings, although inanimate, are to that extent morally superior to men.

John Gloag *'The Significance of Historical Research', in 'Architectural and Industrial Design', a paper read to the Royal Society of Arts (20 March 1963)*

¶72

Architecture arises out of our need to shelter the human animal in a spatial environment and to enclose the social animal in a group space. In this sense architecture serves our institutions and expresses the values of our culture.

Robert Geddes *quoted in 'Contemporary Architects' (1980)*

¶73

There is no finality in architecture, only continuous change.

Walter Gropius *quoted in 'The design of energy-responsive commercial buildings' by Solar Energy Research Unit*

¶74

The basic nature of architecture is in its holes.

Hiroshi Hara *quoted in 'Contemporary Architects' (1980)*

¶75

The transcendence of accommodation is the difference between the art of architecture and building.

Charles Gwathmey *quoted in 'Contemporary Architects' (1980)*

¶76

When you are looking for a solution to what you are told is an architectural problem – remember, it may not be a building.

Ron Herron

¶77

The frolic architecture of the snow.

Ralph Waldo Emerson *'The Snowstorm'*

¶78

The essence of architecture is the inner-relation and interaction of mass, space, place and line. The purpose of architecture is to enrich the joy and drama of living. The spirit of architecture is its truthfulness to itself.

Craig Ellwood *quoted in 'Contemporary Architects' (1980)*

¶79

Architecture is mainly a question of overcoming certain practical problems.

Harald Deilmann *quoted in 'Contemporary Architects' (1980)*

¶80

Architecture, of all the arts, is the one which acts the most slowly, but the most surely, on the soul.

Ernest Dimnett *'What We Live By'*

¶81

Architecture is significant only in its responses to specific needs.

James Cubitt *quoted in 'Contemporary Architects' (1980)*

¶82

Architecture is a social art and only makes sense as the promoter and extender of human relations.

Sir Denys Lasdun *quoted in 'Contemporary Architects' (1980)*

¶83

Architecture is in a sense a microcosm of the city.

Sir Denys Lasdun *'Architecture in an Age of Scepticism' (1984)*

¶84

Architecture [is] a theatre stage setting where the leading actors are the people, and to dramatically direct the dialogue between these people and space is the technique of designing.

Kisho Kurokawa *quoted in 'Contemporary Architects' (1980)*

¶85

Postwar architecture is the accountants' revenge on the prewar businessmen's dreams.

Rem Koolhaas *'Delirious New York' (1978)*

¶86

The duty of the artist is to strain against the bonds of the existing style . . . and only this procedure makes the development of architecture possible.

Philip Johnson *quoted in 'Conversations with Artists' by Selden Rodman*

¶87

Architecture is the art of how to waste space.

Philip Johnson *quoted in 'The New York Times' (1964)*

¶88

I don't believe that architecture is ennobling . . . to me, it's merely a matter of kicks.

Philip Johnson *quoted in 'Esquire' (1974)*

¶89

I've always been for grandeur . . . The history of architecture is the history of monuments. I don't think man lives by bread and bad housing alone.

Philip Johnson (1984)

¶90

All sensible and sensitive people know that modern architecture is bad and horrible.

Paul Johnson

¶91

It's tragic what's happening to architecture. One objects to the ghastly anonymity of it all. You can't name a building by an architect. I know only the names of three modern architects, and I've forgotten those.

Sir Osbert Lancaster *quoted in 'The Times' obituary (29 July 1986)*

¶92

Modern architecture died in St Louis, Missouri, on July 15, 1972 at 3.32pm (or thereabouts) when the infamous Pruitt-Igoe scheme, or rather several of its slab blocks, were given the final coup de grace by dynamite. Previously it had been vandalised, mutilated and defaced by its black inhabitants, and although millions of dollars were pumped back, trying to keep it alive (fixing the broken elevators, repairing smashed windows, repainting), it was finally put out of its misery. Boom, boom, boom.

Dr Charles Jencks *'The Language of Post-Modern Architecture' (Fourth Edition 1984)*

¶93

The surest test of the civilization of a people – at least, as sure as any – afforded by mechanical art is to be found in their architecture, which presents so noble a field for the display of grand and the beautiful, and which, at the same time, is so intimately connected with the essential comforts of life.

Harry S Truman *radio address to delegates at the opening session of the United Nations Conference*

¶94

The art of dancing stands at the source of all the arts that express themselves first in the human person. The art of building, or architecture, is the beginning of all the arts that lie outside the person; and in the end they unite.

Havelock Ellis *'The Dance of Life'*

¶95

Architecture . . . the adaptation of form to resist force.

John Ruskin *'Val d'Arno'*

¶96

Explaining exactly what regional architecture is, might be a job for Jesuits rather than designers.

David Dillon

¶97

To talk of architecture is a joke
Till you can build a chimney that won't smoke.

James Robinson Planche *(paraphrasing Aristophanes, The Birds, l 1034)*

The Professionals

¶98

Life is the gift of the immortal gods, living well is the gift of philosophy. Was it philosophy that erected all the towering tenements, so dangerous to the persons who dwell in them? Believe me, that was a happy age, before the days of architects, before the days of builders.

Seneca (*c*.4 BC to AD65) *in a letter to Lucilius*

¶99

All professions are conspiracies against the laity.

George Bernard Shaw *'The Doctor's Dilemma'*

¶100

Definition of an architect: A self-made man who worships his creator.

Richard England

¶101

Definition of a consultant – someone called in to share the blame.

Dr John Parker

¶102

Lawyer – have we left anything out?
Surgeon – have we left anything in?
Architect – have we anything left?

Anon

¶103

Architect, n. One who drafts a plan of your house, and plans a draft of your money.

Ambrose Bierce 'The Devil's Dictionary'

¶104

The architect must produce something that is visually beautiful as well as socially useful.

HRH The Prince of Wales addressing architects at Hampton Court Palace (1984)

¶105

Architects, along with planners (with whom they merge), intellectual disciples of Keynes and the general secretaries of trade unions, are presently prominent in the class of scapegoats, about whom nothing too harsh can be said since they are held responsible for everything which discontents us.

Prince among architects leading article in 'The Times' (1 June 1984)

¶106

A lawyer without history or literature is a mechanic, a mere working mason; if he possesses some knowledge of these, he may venture to call himself an architect.

Sir Walter Scott

¶107

The brevity of human life gives a melancholy to the profession of the architect.

Ralph Waldo Emerson 'Journals' (1842)

¶108

In the hierarchy of the arts it is obviously the architect who is the boss.

Eric Gill

¶109

To spot the expert, pick the one who predicts the job will take longest and cost the most.

Earl Warren quoted in 'Murphy's Law Book Two' by A. Bloch (1980)

¶110

... one who, with a sure and marvellous reason and rule, knows first how to divide things with his mind and intelligence; secondly how to put together in the execution of the work all those materials which, by the movements of weights and the joining and heaping up of bodies, may serve successfully and with dignity, the needs of man.

Leone Battista Alberti

¶111

When engineers and quantity surveyors discuss aesthetics, and architects study what cranes can do, we are on the right road.

Sir Ove Arup quoted in 'Contemporary Architects' (1980)

¶112

The man who builds a factory builds a temple; the man who works there worships there.

Calvin Coolidge

¶113

When I was at the Bar many years ago, a story was told about a famous judge. I believe it was true, but I can't be sure. Mr Justice Pollock frequently heard cases in which expert witnesses gave evidence, and his brother, Freddie, a consulting engineer, frequently gave expert evidence. At some social function, someone asked the judge to define the expression 'expert witness'. The judge thought for a moment and then said: 'There are three categories of expert witnesses – liars, bloody liars, and my brother Freddie.'

Sir Arthur Grattan-Bellow QC *formerly a legal adviser at the Foreign & Commonwealth Office*

¶114

Architects as a profession have a way of oscillating between extreme orgies of breast-beating and of ritual hand-raising.

Tony Aldous

¶115

The architect, as we think of him today, is a tragic hero, a sort of fallen Michaelangelo. He has built too high and has been guilty of hubris.

Nicholas Bagnall *'Fallen angels' book review in the 'Sunday Telegraph' (1983)*

¶116

An expert is a man who has stopped thinking. Why should he think? He is an expert.

Frank Lloyd Wright *quoted in the 'Daily Express' (1959)*

¶117

Every profession has its secrets . . . if it hadn't it wouldn't be a profession.

Saki (H H Munro) *'The Story of St Vespauluus' (1911)*

¶118

No person who is not a great sculptor or painter can be an architect. If he is not a sculptor or a painter, he can only be a builder.

John Ruskin *'Lectures on Architecture and Painting'*

¶119

A consultant is someone who will take your watch off your wrist and tell you what time it is.

Dr David Owen

¶120

If a civil engineer tries to do an architect's work the result is horrifying. If an architect tries to do an engineer's work the result is terrifying.

Old Saying *used by Sir Harold Harding, an engineer, in a letter to 'The Times' (April Fool's Day 1985)*

¶121

'Architectress': of director, directress. A female architect.

Oxford English Dictionary

¶122

Architects are 2% gentlemen and 98% renegade car salesmen.

Stained glass artist *quoted by Byron Rogers in an interview*

¶123

What the modern architect has really done is to revolt against forms of construction which have become so conventional, so conceptualised, that they are like the dead phrases which no poet can use again, clichés like the ambient air, the silver stream, the vast deep, the trackless wild. These have become conceptual forms, standard decorations, pieces of fustian, which actually hide the original intuition, true and powerful, of air, sea, and desert.

Joyce Cary *'Art and Reality'*

¶124

To justify and enhance their superior status, architects feel called upon to make impressive statements. Consequently to speak in such circles of conservation and modest infiltration can be to evoke a kind of castration complex of the sort that afflicts an army when it has to hand in its arms.

Lionel Brett, Viscount Esher *'Parameters and Images: Architecture in a Crowded World' (1980)*

¶125

We are now at the close of one epoch and well before the start of a new one. During this period of transition there will be no moratorium on building, and for obvious reasons. There will just be more architecture without architects.

Peter Blake (1974)

¶126

It only confirmed an early impression of his that Architects were queer people – rather like artists and poets in some ways, but with a basis of bricks and mortar to them.

G K Chesterton

¶127

For far too long, it seems to me, some planners and architects have consistently ignored the feelings and wishes of the mass of ordinary people in this country . . . To be concerned about the way people live; about the environment they inhabit and the kind of community that is created by that environment should surely be one of the prime requirements of a really good architect.

HRH The Prince of Wales *addressing architects at Hampton Court Palace (1984)*

¶128

If architects have a professional future at all it is (in the phrase of Geoffrey Vickers) as 'skilled understanders enabling people to work out their problems'.

Colin Ward *addressing architectural students in Sheffield (1976)*

¶129

What I find most interesting about the new range of architectural heroes is that they are thought important for the process rather than the product. It is the way they go about their work which excites rather than the formal qualities of their work . . . When Jim Johnson took me to the original ASSIST shop in the Govan Road, everybody in the street greeted him with a smile. Does this happen to the local authority architect inspecting an improvement area?

Colin Ward (1978)

¶130

What I believe is important about Community Architecture is that it has shown 'ordinary' people that their views are worth having; that architects and planners do not necessarily have the monopoly of knowing best about taste, style and planning; that they need not be made to feel guilty or ignorant if their natural preference is for the more 'traditional' designs – for a small garden, for courtyards, arches and porches – and there is a growing number of architects prepared to listen and to offer imaginative ideas.

HRH The Prince of Wales *addressing architects at Hampton Court Palace (1984)*

¶131

Owing to such things as town planning hurdles it is perhaps not surprising that buildings tend to be designed not to give delight, but to achieve minimum displeasure. There may be an understandable fear of architects and the jargon they use to convince you of your unutterable ignorance is decidedly off-putting for a potential patron. What we need now, therefore, are many more people refusing to be put off and demanding a creative dialogue between the architect and patron where both truly care about the quality of the end product. Only then will we see a reawakening of the patron's sense of responsibility, in that the results of his work will have an impact on the many people who use, live alongside or simply pass the building. Good architecture is not a luxury, nor need it be more expensive. Developers are coming to realise that good design produces a sound investment, while good patrons produce even better architects.

HRH The Prince of Wales *addressing the Institute of Directors' annual convention (1985)*

¶132

When he walked in wearing that bow tie we thought he was the editor of an architectural magazine.

PR person *commenting on the Editor, 'Business Systems & Equipment' (July/August 1986)*

¶133

Few people like architects. Fewer still perhaps like journalists. Both, in the public eye, share to an equal degree the faults of incompetence and vanity. It might therefore be thought that the architectural journalist would by his profession suffer a double odium. This, however unjust, might be true if he were more often encountered or more widely read. The truth is that he is a rare bird, and the layman normally takes only a superficial interest – if any at all – in what he writes. Architectural journalism is still written largely for architects, and the battles, however ruthless, and the games, however childish, are mostly domestic ones. This does not mean that they are not serious or important to the participants.

Sir Hugh Casson (1968)

¶134

An architect requires a great many men to erect his building. But he does not ask them to vote on his design. They work together by free agreement and each is free in his proper function. An architect uses steel, glass, concrete produced by others. But the materials remain just so much steel, glass and concrete until he touches them.

Ayn Rand's *character Howard Roark, quoted in 'The Fountainhead' (1947)*

¶135

The only thing worse than working with architects is working without them.

Dr John Parker

¶136

The warmth and directness with which ages of crafts and a more personal relation between architect and client endowed buildings of the past may have gone for good. The architect, to represent this century of ours, must be colder, cold to keep in command of mechanized production, cold to design for the satisfaction of anonymous clients.

Sir Nikolaus Pevsner *'Pioneers of Modern Design' (1960)*

¶137

Admiring enter'd and the work some praise,
And some the architect.

John Milton *'Paradise Lost', Bk i (1730)*

¶138

We must ask the bat-eyed priests of technology what on earth they think they are doing.

Lewis Mumford

¶139

The self-sufficiency of the specialist's world is a prisoner's illusion. It is time to open the gates.

Lewis Mumford

¶140

In the two short centuries since architecture has become a well-defined profession of its own, its identity has afforded endless controversy. Is it an art practised by and for the sake of individuals, or a commercial enterprise geared to the needs of the market and the generation of profit, or a communal under-taking dedicated to the service of society?

Most enquirers rash enough to essay a serious answer to these questions have ended in admitting compromise – each or some of these ideas have a place in the best architecture. Architecture, if it is to go beyond the drawings board, is divided from the disciplines with which it is most often compared, the other 'arts', by the need to compromise, by the insistent demands of what is real and what is practical. Before these obligations all transcendent principles of 'truth' in archi-tecture will always fall down. A compromise of ideals lies at the heart of the matter, to the chagrin of the pure in soul.

Andrew Saint *'The Image of the Architect' (1983)*

¶141

The best of British architecture is as good as any in the world. But that best does not often come from the top of the professional establishment or the front of the avant-garde: it is more likely to be done in the obscurity of a county architect's office or by a small provincial firm which really cares about the needs of its clients and the permanence of its finishes.

Iain Nairn

¶142

If architecture is to be of service, it must respond to more than need. The architect must also serve desire; the desire of the building to be what it wants to be and the desire of the human being for self-expression. In serving desire, architecture contributes to the spiritual enrichment of the world.

John Lobell *'Between Silence and Light: Spirit in the Architecture of Louis I. Kahn' (1979)*

¶143

After consulting all the pundits, however exalted or however humble, architects will not be able to evade their responsibility to create an architecture that evokes the promise, and so provokes the action, for a more sane society to come. Only then are they more likely to receive the confidence and respect of the public community they so assiduously seek.

Berthold Lubetkin *RIBA President's invitation lecture (1985)*

¶144

No one who follows others can ever get in front of them, and those who can't do good work on their own account can hardly make good use of what others have done.

Michelangelo Buonarroti

¶145

If it ain't broke, don't fix it – unless you are a consultant.

Winston G Rossiter

¶146

Architects never felt the urge to establish ethical precepts for the performance of their profession, as did the medical fraternity. No equivalent of the Hippocratic oath exists for them. Hippocrates' promise that 'the regimen I adopt shall be for the benefit of my patients according to my ability and judgement, and not for their hurt or for any wrong' has no counterpart in their book. Criticism within the profession – the only conceivable way to spread a sense of responsibility among its members – is tabooed by their own codified standards of practice. To bolster their own ego, architects hold their own beauty contests, award each other prizes, decorate each other with gold medals, and make light of the damning fact that they do not amount to any moral force in this country. The situation is not altogether new. 'No profession has done its duty until it has furnished a victim,' said Disraeli; '. . . suppose an architect were hanged. Terror has its aspiration, as well as competition.'

Bernard Rudofsky *'Streets for People: A Primer for Americans' (1969)*

¶147

It is worthy of note that most of the famous Roman architects were engineers.

W R Lethaby

¶148

For painters, poets and builders have very high flights, but they must be kept down.

Sarah, 1st Duchess of Marlborough *letter to the Duchess of Bedford (21 June 1734)*

¶149

Very few architects know anything about architecture. For 500 years architecture has been a phoney.

Frank Lloyd Wright *quoted in the 'Daily Express' (1959)*

¶150

For architects just happen to be the handmaidens of the speculators who work toward 'the death of the city by development'. The phrase is Ada Louise Huxtable's, New York's guardian angel without portfolio, and architecture critic of the Times. Are the harsh words justifiable? Or could it be that we are mis-reading the profoundest thoughts of those architects who give aid and comfort (in the form of drawings and specifications) to the vilest schemes of the developers? Architects probably have known all along that the demise of

American cities is inevitable, and content themselves with practising urban euthenasia. At all events, their callous kiss of death pays off handsomely. 'Human amenities? Urban aesthetics? Public good?' asks Mrs Huxtable. 'None of it balances against private profit.'

Bernard Rudofsky *'Streets for People: A Primer for Americans' (1969)*

¶151

The best lack all conviction, while the worst are full of passionate intensity.

W B Yeats

¶152

Architects vary like doctors and lawyers, some are good – some bad. Unfortunately, in architecture, failure shows.

Peter Shepherd *former President of the RIBA*

¶153

It is astonishing with what savagery planners and architects are trying to obliterate working-class cultural and social patterns. Is it because many of them are first generation middle-class technosnobs?

Bruce Allsopp *'Towards a Humane Architecture' (1974)*

¶154

A good architect can make an old house look a lot better by just discussing the cost of a new one.

Anon

¶155

Architecture as now practised is in some sense a largely discredited profession. Thus a great many people are clearly of the view that any proposed new building whether in Whitehall or in the village high street, is bound to be worse than whatever it replaces. What people object to in modern architecture is its coarse inhumanity, its crude materials, its graceless unadorned bulk (the exteriors too high and the interiors too low), the restless insecurity of its 'flexible' open planning, and the absence of 'finish', of craftsmanship and of mouldings, those civilizing lines that guide and reassure the eye in other types of building.

Dr David Watkin *in 'The Times' (1 March 1973)*

¶156

Truman's Law: If you can't convince them, confuse them.

Harry S Truman

¶157

All reformers, however strict their social conscience, live in houses just as big as they can pay for.

Logan Pearsall Smith

¶158

The business of the architect is to make the designs and estimates, to direct the works, and to measure and value the different parts; he is the intermediate agent between the employer, whose honour and interest he is to study, and the mechanic, whose rights he is to defend. His situation implies great trust; he is responsible for the mistakes, negligences, and ignorances of those he employs; and above all, he is to take care that the workmen's bills do not exceed his own estimates. If these are the duties of an architect, with what propriety can his situation, and that of the builder, or the contractor, be united?

Sir John Soane *'Plans, Elevations and Sections of Buildings' (1788)*

¶159

Architects' president Owen Luder recently praised one of the designs for the National Gallery extension on the grounds that the message it conveyed was: 'Sod off!'

A rather weird attitude, you might think – but one – it turns out, that Mr Luder expressed in a Southwark context almost 20 years ago.

Of the Acorn estate in Peckham he wrote in the South London Press in 1965:

'It is a revolutionary estate admired by architects and planners from all over the world but criticised and even reviled by the tenants themselves who have become obsessed with the teething troubles of the central heating system and the more domestic changes they have to make when moving from more conventional homes.

Tenants are simply not educated into taking pride in living in adventurous new estates designed for 20th century living rather than carrying on their humdrum normal existence in worthy but immensely dull boxes of bricks.'

So now we know: it's all the TENANTS' fault.

Bob Smyth

¶160

Life is rich, always changing, always challenging, and we architects have the task of transmitting into wood, concrete, glass and steel, of transforming human aspirations into habitable and meaningful space.

Arthur Erickson *quoted in 'Contemporary Architects' (1980)*

¶161

The planner is my shepherd. He maketh me to walk; through dark tunnels and underpasses he forceth me to go. He maketh concrete canyons tower above me. By the rivers of traffic he maketh me walk. He knocketh down all that is good, he maketh straight the curves. He maketh of the city a wasteland and a car park.

Mike Harding *in 'A Short Guide to Modern Architecture', 'When the Martians Land in Huddersfield' (1984)*

¶162

Men who love building are their own undoers, and need no other enemies.

Marcus Crassus *'Plutarch, Lives'*

¶163

First Clown: What is he that builds stronger than the mason, the shipwright, or the carpenter?

Second Clown: The gallows-maker; for that frame outlives a thousand tenants.

William Shakespeare *'Hamlet'*

¶164

A man who could build a church, as one may say, by squinting at a sheet of paper.

Charles Dickens *'Martin Chuzzelwit'*

¶165

Q: Why are property developers like starlings?

A: Because they eat in the country and shit in the city.

Louis Kahn *(attributed to)*

¶166

Q: Why is a spec builder's architect like a ham actor?

A: Because they both draw poor houses.

Louis Hellman

¶167

Planners and architects are hooked on objects, and long for stable societies, for correct and accepted precedent within which a professional performance can be judged and applauded.

Theo Crosby *'How to Play the Environment Game' (1973)*

¶168

That which distils, preserves and then enlarges the experience of a people is literature: and though I do not seek to absolve architects of their misdemeanours, I submit this thesis that with kitchen sink literature, it was natural that kitchen sink architecture would follow. If you seek their monument just look around you.

H D F Kitto *'The Greeks'*

¶169

We're having a lot of fun. Now you can say it's much better to build higher buildings for the greater glory of God than it is for the greater glory of Mammon, but that isn't what we think now.

Philip Johnson (1984)

¶170

The architect is the servant of society, of the style and of the mores, of the baits, of the customs, of the demands, of the time in which he works.

Philip Johnson *quoted in 'Esquire' (1974)*

¶171

Life (for an architect) begins at 45.

Philip Johnson *when he was 70*

¶172

The architectural horrors with which the public is often confronted are not merely due to the incompetence of architects, but to the crumbling civilisation in which we live. After all, what is the visual equivalent of a world that allows 40,000 children to die needlessly each day, while the United States of America alone spends $26 million an hour on armaments?

Berthold Lubetkin *RIBA President's invitation lecture (1985)*

¶173

There still remains the architect's role to be assessed in connection with the urban nightmare. Despite an uninterrupted record of bungled cities, Americans have preserved a touching faith in the practitioners of architecture. This faith, unshaken by experience, is no doubt a residue from the time when architects were the prodigies of the human race, combining in one person the talents and skills of sculptor, painter and writer. (Le Corbusier was the last of this tribe of complete artists.) Perhaps also the transferred uses of the word architect – as the spiritual parent of a scheme – brought a certain loftiness to it. Not that architects ever ranked among national heroes. Far from it. They are one of the least conspicuous professional groups. Artists' and writers' names may become household words, but not architects'. Architects rarely make headlines, and then only in the Sunday supplements of metropolitan newspapers.

Bernard Rudofsky *'Streets for People: A Primer for Americans' (1969)*

¶174

You've been taken on as Land Surveyor, as you say, but, unfortunately, we have no need of a Land Surveyor. There wouldn't be the least use for one here. The frontiers of our little state are marked out and all officially recorded.

Franz Kafka *'The Castle'*

¶175

The singing masons building roofs of gold.

William Shakespeare *'Henry V' Act 1 sc ii*

¶176

A doctor, an architect and a politician argued as to whose was the oldest profession.

'Obviously, the medical profession is the oldest,' said the doctor, 'since the first doctor was the one who took the rib out of Adam to create Eve.'

The architect disagreed. 'The first architect created order out of chaos in the firmament, so mine must be the oldest profession.'

'Ah!' said the politician, 'But it was the first politician who created the chaos!'

Tam Dalyell MP *in an after-dinner story*

¶177

About 11 years ago my son Ben and his friend Patrick, then both aged 4, were doing some 'building' in the garden.

Ben – 'What we need is an Architect.'

Patrick – 'What is an Architect?'

Ben – 'I'm not sure but I think it's a type of screwdriver.'

Perry Sennitt

People

¶178
Sir Christopher Wren
Said, 'I am going to dine with some men.
If anybody calls
Say I am designing St Paul's.'
   Edmund Clerihew Bentley

¶179
That miracle of a youth, Mr. Christopher Wren.
   John Evelyn *'Diary'* *(11 July 1654)*

¶180
Though I've always considered Sir Christopher Wren,
As an architect, one of the greatest of men;
And, talking of Epitaphs, – much I admire his,
'Circumspice, si Monumentum requiris';
Which an erudite Verger translated to me,
'If you ask for his Monument, Sir-come-spy-see!'
   The Reverend R H Barham *'The Cynotaph'*

¶181
An English peer invited Franklin, during his stay in London, to admire a house
the peer had recently had built for himself. Behind the handsome colonnaded
façade, the house was oddly and inconveniently laid out on account of the narrow

and irregular plot on which it had been constructed. 'All you need to do to enjoy your house, my lord,' Franklin observed, 'is to rent a spacious apartment directly across the street.'

Benjamin Franklin

¶182
He's a real nowhere man,
Sitting in his nowhere land,
Making all his nowhere plans for nobody.

Lennon & McCartney *'Nowhere Man' – song*

¶183
When in June 1906 Harry Thaw shot the well-known architect Stanford White in a quarrel over Evelyn Nesbit, the scandal gripped the entire country. Some years later Wilson Mizner, observing with distaste a Palm Beach hotel designed by Joseph Urban, remarked 'Harry Thaw shot the wrong architect'.

Wilson Mizner *[this remark has been ascribed to others about other architects.]*

¶184
The youth gets together his materials to build a bridge to the moon, or perchance, a palace or temple on the earth and, at length, the middle-aged man concludes to build a woodshed with them.

Henry David Thoreau *'Journal'*

¶185
The brazen plate upon the door (which being Mr Pecksniff's, could not lie) bore this inscription. PECKSNIFF, ARCHITECT, to which Mr Pecksniff, on his cards of business added, AND LAND SURVEYOR. In one sense, and only one, he may be said to have been a Land Surveyor on a pretty large scale, as an extensive prospect lay stretched out before the windows of his house. Of his architectural doings, nothing was clearly known, except that he had never designed or built anything; but it was generally understood that his knowledge of the science was almost awful in its profoundity.

Charles Dickens *'Martin Chuzzlewit'*

¶186
He paints like an architect and builds like a painter.

Anon *of Karl Friedrich Schinkel*

¶187
In the heyday of his career as art critic, Ruskin used always to maintain that it should in no way affect his friendship with an artist if he panned his work. The artists, of course, saw matters in a rather different light. 'Next time I meet you I shall knock you down,' one of his victims retorted, 'but I trust it will make no difference to our friendship.'

John Ruskin

¶188

Mendelsohn's genius was to be able to make his buildings look like his first sketches.

Serge Chermayeff

¶189

I had to choose between honest arrogance or hypocritical humility. I chose honest arrogance.

Frank Lloyd Wright

¶190

In 1930 novelist Rex Stout built a fourteen-room house, with his own hands, on a hilltop in Danbury, Connecticut. Later he invited Frank Lloyd Wright out to see it and waited patiently for his evaluation. Wright examined it carefully and then said, 'A superb spot. Someone should build a house here.'

Frank Lloyd Wright

¶191

In 1937, Wright built a house in Wisconsin for industrialist Hibbard Johnson and his family. One rainy evening Johnson was entertaining some distinguished guests for dinner when the roof began to leak. The water seeped through the ceiling directly above Johnson himself, dripping steadily onto the top of his bald head. Irate, he put a call through to Wright in Phoenix, Arizona. 'Frank,' he said, 'you built this beautiful house for me and we enjoy it very much. But I have told you the roof leaks, and right now I am with some friends and distinguished guests and it is leaking right on top of my head.' Wright's reply was heard by all. 'Well Hib,' he said, 'why don't you move your chair?'

*(This anecdote is told by **Samuel C Johnson**, a member of the Johnson family, famous wax manufacturers. It appears in a brochure issued by the Johnson Foundation.)*

¶192

There is nothing so frightening as a million dollars.

Frank Lloyd Wright

¶193

Sir Edwin Lutyens was without any doubt the greatest folly builder England has ever seen.

Sir Nikolaus Pevsner *'Building with Wit', in 'Architectural Review' (April 1954)*

¶194

Lutyens introduced to a clergyman named Western – 'Any relation to the Great Western?'

Sir Edwin Lutyens

¶195

Banister Fletcher receiving guests at a RIBA reception: . . .
'I'm Maufe'
'Oh my dear chap you can't, we are only just starting.'

Geoffrey Barnsley

¶196

I see no reason to invent a new architecture every Monday morning. I don't want to be interesting – I want to be good.

Ludwig Mies van der Rohe *quoted in 'The Sunday Times' (1971)*

¶197

Mies van der Rohe did not believe that an architect should indulge in self-expression. Once a student asked him for his opinion of this subject. He handed her a pencil and paper and told her to write her name. When she had done so, he said, 'That's for self-expression. Now we get to work.'

Ludwig Mies van der Rohe

¶198

The eighteenth century having posited the fundamental principles of reason, the nineteenth, in a magnificent effort of work, plunged into analysis and experiment and created a completely new tool, formidable, revolutionary and revolutionising society. Inheritors of this effort, we perceive the modern age and we feel an epoch of creation is about to begin.

Le Corbusier *'Urbanisme' (1924)*

¶199

I myself am installed in a windowless air-conditioned office, a kind of cell. My visitors are conscious of this fact, which makes them speak concisely and to the point. I have had as many as four come to see me at a time.

Le Corbusier

¶200

With a ruthless disregard for tradition, but a deep respect for human values, Le Corbusier has evolved forms suited to 20th century living.

Terence Mullaly *in 'The Daily Telegraph' (4 February 1959)*

¶201

Karl Marx suffered from the same kind of illusions as poor Le Corbusier, whose recent death filled me with immense joy. Both of them were architects. Le Corbusier was a pitiable creature working in reinforced concrete. Mankind will soon be landing on the moon, and just imagine: that buffoon claimed we'd be taking along sacks of reinforced concrete. His heaviness and the heaviness of the concrete deserve one another . . . Le Corbusier simply went down for the third time [when he drowned in 1965], because of his reinforced concrete and his architectures, the ugliest and most unacceptable buildings in the world. All the same, if God exists, He'd expect me to act like a gentleman. So I ordered some everlasting flowers for the anniversary of his death, next year, and I cried out: 'Long live anti-gravitation.'

Salvador Dali *quoted in 'Conversations with Dali' by Alan Bosquet (1969)*

¶202

To blame Le Corbusier for Ronan Point is like blaming Mozart for Muzak.

Sam Webb *on the eighteenth anniversary of the collapse of Ronan Point (16 May 1986)*

¶203

Vincent Harris receiving the Royal Gold Medal – 'Look, a lot of you people here tonight don't like what I do and I don't like what a lot of you do, but I am proud and honoured to receive the Royal Gold Medal.'

Arthur Bailey *in 'The Times' obituary (12 August 1971)*

¶204

Alberti recommends that churches should be white, not on grounds of taste, but because 'purity and simplicity of colour, as of life, is most pleasing to God.'

Leone Battista Alberti

¶205

The sun never knew how wonderful it was until it shone on the wall of a building.

Louis Kahn

¶206

I think joy is the key word in our work.

Louis Kahn

¶207

A school is two men talking under a tree.

Louis Kahn

¶208

Architecture does not exist. What does exist is the *work* of architecture.

Louis Kahn

¶209

Modern man is born in a clinic and dies in a clinic. It is therefore not surprising that he should spend the intermediate period between these two paramount events of his life in utterly soulless clinical environments.

Richard England *quoted in 'Contemporary Architects' (1980)*

¶210

I know of no safe depository of the ultimate powers of society but the people themselves: and if we think them not enlightened enough to exercise their control with a wholesome discretion, the remedy is not to take it from them, but to inform their discretion.

Thomas Jefferson *US President (1801–9) and architect*

¶211

The most important thing about it is the power to the people bit. In general, in Liverpool people are told what they are getting, not asked what they want. But once we had established our viability by being accepted by the government for funding, we determined everything; the way we lived, and who we employed to run our affairs. We did not succumb to bureaucracy.

We got the architects and builders and everybody else on our terms. We told them what we wanted and consulted right the way through, from day one, at every stage. Through the design committee we decided on every single aspect of the scheme right down to the sort of trees we planted.

We've proved to the council and government and anybody else listening that if people are given the reins, get the right help and are committed, they can come up with a really excellent viable housing scheme that people *want* to live in.

Alan Hoyte *first chairman of Hesketh Street Co-operative, Liverpool (1984)*

¶212

Doing it yourself is also instructive, practically and in arousing empathy with builders, and in that it must constitute the opposite process to the totally understandable advice that I believe Alberti gave; that the architect should never visit the site of his building while under construction, lest sympathy with the problems experienced by the builder should lead him to modify the purity of the design. In this Alberti, humanist though he was, stressed the cerebral part of the art of building; my early experience stressed the sensual or tactile.

Edward Cullinan *'Building Them Yourself', in 'Edward Cullinan Architects' (1984)*

¶213

No monopoly of virtue exists as between public or private monopolies.

Professor Sir George Grenfell-Baines *'Thoughts occurring to one during fifty years of practice' (1986)*

¶214

Enterprise is found in individuals or small groups.
Enterprise does not readily spread. Public enterprise is a myth.

Professor Sir George Grenfell-Baines *'Thoughts occurring to one during fifty years in practice' (1986)*

¶215

Too low they build, who build beneath the stars.

Edward Young *'Night'*

Hellmanisms

¶216

The priests of Mesopotamia,
Were architects in their spare tamia,
The plans it seems,
They received in their dreams,
Straight from God, just like (I leave you to fill in the namia).

¶217

Philip Johnson, all heil!
Invented the International Style,
Now he's had to change his spots,
In order to maintain his yachts!

¶218

They say the young Charles Rennie Mackintosh,
Was a dab hand at the Art Nouveau colour wash,
His designs seem to transcend mere bricks and mortar,
Probably because he used Scotch instead of water!

¶219

Frank Lloyd Wright on the prairie,
Came on like some nutty old fairy,
And in the city he got positively manic,
Always threatening to do something organic.

¶220

At the Bauhaus, Walter Gropius was the hub,
Later on he designed the Playboy Club,
Quite a change from cones, spheres and cubes,
Building for Bunnies with big bums and boobs!

¶221

Ludwig Mies van der Rohe,
Detailed the Seagram you know,
On two A4 sheets if you please,
Well, less drawings, more fees!

¶222

Ludwig Mies van der Rohe,
Designed chairs incredibly low,
Probably because his arse,
Was made of steel and glass!

¶223
Corb in his youth was Mr Clean,
A house to him was just a machine,
And when the clients started to grouse,
He redesigned them to fit the house!

¶224
An architect went up to heaven and rejoiced,
'Isn't that Corb I see over there?', he voiced,
'No, that's God,' he heard St Peter say,
'He just thinks He's Le Corbusier.'

¶225
Alvar Aalto didn't say much,
No cant, jargon or double Dutch,
But his surfaces will never diminish,
They're what you might call 'double Finnish'!

¶226
We can do almost anything,
We could go on a moon mission,
Only thing we can't do,
Is get a commission.
on Archigram

¶227
Norman Foster, king of High Tech,
Has got tubular steel for a neck,
It's a pity his brain can't be seen,
It's made entirely of neoprene!

¶228
Richard Rogers has lots of guts, there's no doubt,
If you go to the Lloyd's Building you can see them all hanging out,
All the plumbing's exposed, it's terribly organic,
Uncompromisingly High Tech, just like the Titanic,
For architects and students and journalists it's a must,
(Let's hope the owners are well insured against rust!)

¶229
Big Jim had a Stirling crisis,
It was by the Cam, not the Isis,
When the library gave him a nasty turn,
Called Post-Modern-Classic-change-of-heart burn.

¶230
Terry Farrell designed a wall,
Terry Farrell says it all,
When asked what it means, he says, and I quote,
'It's not eggsplicit, it's just a yoke!'

¶231
For Michael Graves life must be pretty hectic,
It's damn difficult being that eclectic,
Dissecting dead styles is his totem,
Not so much Post Modern as post mortem.

¶232
Charlie Moore came to town,
To prove he was no phony,
So he left a piazza there,
Made of macaroni!

¶233
Bruce Goff was a bit of a loner,
Possibly because he hailed from Oklahoma,
And thought architecture should be fun,
Sort of 'Annie Get Your Mastic Gun'.

¶234
The Spaniard Ricardo Bofill,
Builds Pseudo-Classical French overspill,
The proles, you should see 'em,
Love living in a Colosseum,
Shouting 'Hail Mitterand, thumbs down and kill!'

¶235
Leon Krier,
Adores Albert Speer,
He wants to turn Ally Pally,
Into a Nuremberg rally!

¶236
Aldo Rossi,
Is a dead lossi,
He's certainly notta,
Mario Botta.

¶237
Venturi in dark coloured specs,
Went to Las Vegas for sex,
He started off raw,
But learned from a whore,
Acts contradictory and complex!

Theory

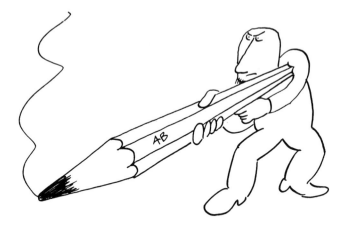

¶238
Architectural power grows out of the barrel of a 4b pencil.
Dr Charles Jencks *after Mao Tse-Tung*

¶239
Too many stairs and back-doors make thieves and whores.
Balthazar Gerbier *'Discourse on Building' ch14 (1662)*

¶240
A postern door makes thief and whore.
William Camden *'Remains'*

¶241
We shape our buildings, thereafter they shape us.
Sir Winston Churchill *quoted in 'Time' (1960)*

¶242
We shape our tools and thereafter they shape us.
Father John Culkin SJ *'A Handful of Postulates' (1966)*

¶243
Form follows function.
Louis Sullivan *(1895)*

¶244
Small rooms or dwellings discipline the mind, large ones weaken it.
Leonardo da Vinci '*Notebooks*' *(c.1500)*

¶245
The assumption that the specialists know better drags theory and practice into the bog of reactionary cosmopolitan opinion. The proletariat acquired the right to have their Corinthian colonnades.
Joseph Stalin

¶246
When they come downstairs from their ivory towers, idealists are apt to walk straight into the gutter.
Logan Pearsall Smith

¶247
The reality of the building consisted not in the four walls and the roof but in the space within.
Lao Tzu

¶248
An arch never sleeps.
James Fergusson *repeating a Hindu aphorism*

¶249
The object of art is to give life a shape.
Jean Anhouilh '*The Rehearsal*', *Act I Sc ii (1960)*

¶250
A building or a space should make one feel that a thought is within it, that it is more than a shelter, as a good book is more than words put together, as music is more than an arrangement of notes.
Max Abranovitz *quoted in 'Contemporary Architects' (1980)*

¶251
The creative artist is by nature and by office the qualified leader in any society, natural, native interpreter of the visible form of any social order in or under which we choose to live.
Frank Lloyd Wright *(1935)*

¶252
We are all victims of the rectangle and the slab. We go on living in boxes of stone and brick while the modern world is dying to be born in the discovery that concrete and steel can sleep together.
Frank Lloyd Wright *quoted in 'Manchester Guardian' (1959)*

¶253

A doctor can bury his mistakes, but an architect can only advise his client to plant vines.

Frank Lloyd Wright *quoted in 'The Sunday Times' (1957)*

¶254

Make no little plans; they have no magic to stir men's blood.

Daniel Hudson Burnham

¶255

The demand that all buildings should become works of architecture . . . is strictly offensive to common sense . . . One might possibly stipulate that architecture is a social institution related to building in much the same way that literature is to speech.

Colin Rowe *'Collage City' (1978)*

¶256

When things are built they should be put in mothballs.

Philip Johnson *quoted in 'Esquire' (1974)*

¶257

Perhaps the blank faceless abstract quality of our modern architecture is a reflection of the anxiety we feel before the void, a kind of visual static which emanates from the psyche of us all, as if we do not know which way to go.

Norman Mailer *'Cannibals and Christians'*

¶258

Thus when we view some well-proportion'd dome . . .
No single parts inequally surprise,
All comes united to th'admiring eyes.

Alexander Pope *'Essay on Criticism', Pt ii l 47*

¶259

The fundamental failure of modern architecture was that in the shift from an agrarian society to an industrialised society, from handicrafts to the machine, from single production to mass production, in trying to produce in abundance for all the people, the people themselves got left out.

John Portman *(1984)*

¶260

What distinguishes architecture from painting and sculpture is its spatial quality. In this, and only in this, no other artist can emulate the architect. Thus the history of architecture is primarily a history of man shaping space, and the historian must keep spatial problems always in the foreground.

Sir Nikolaus Pevsner *'An Outline of European Architecture' (1943)*

¶261

To fight against the shoddy design of those goods by which our fellow-men are surrounded becomes a moral duty.

Sir Nikolaus Pevsner 'Industrial Art in England'

¶262

No architecture is so haughty as that which is simple.

John Ruskin 'Stones of Venice', Vol ii ch 6 sec 73

¶263

Better the rudest work that tells a story or records a fact, than the richest without meaning. There should not be a single ornament put upon great civic buildings, without some intellectual intention.

John Ruskin 'The Lamp of Memory'

¶264

The great Puritan experiment to discover the limits of human capacity for taking punishment has not benefited mankind as expected. Anybody who is able to perceive the wretchedness of our way of life and the containers who shape it will want to strive for a more dignified existence. The difficulty lies in finding a way out of our mental slump.

Bernard Rudofsky 'The Prodigious Builders' (1977)

¶265

Great art . . . is preeminently and finally the expression of the spirits of great men.

John Ruskin 'Modern Painters' (1843–60)

¶266

As architecture proliferated, it lost its integrity. At one point some of it succumbed to perpetual progress, never to recover . . . [from] the progressive-aggressive profession whose unattractive products are uppermost in our mind, if only for their inherent uppishness.

Bernard Rudofsky 'The Prodigious Builders' (1977)

¶267

Whatever ornaments we admit ought clearly to be of a chaste, grave and noble kind: and what furniture we employ, evidently more for the honouring of God's word than for the ease of the preacher.

John Ruskin 'On Pulpits'

¶268

We require from buildings, as from men, two kinds of goodness: first, the doing their practical duty well: then that they be graceful and pleasing in doing it; which last is itself another form of duty.

John Ruskin 'Stones of Venice', Vol i ch 2

¶269
When we build, let us think that we build for ever.
   John Ruskin *'The Seven Lamps of Architecture' (1849)*

¶270
We must give up designing the broken-down picturesque which is part of the ideal of make-believe. The enemy is not science but vulgarity, a pretence to beauty at second hand.
   W R Lethaby

¶271
To build is to be robbed.
   Samuel Johnson *'The Idler' No. 62*

¶272
The building of tall blocks without any intrinsic message (they are merely units of accommodation) devalues the identity of the city and robs it of meaningful symbols. In a mass society the identity of the individual is a precious responsibility, to be reinforced at every stage.
   Theo Crosby *'How to Play the Environment Game' (1973)*

¶273
Given the trend of our age to eliminate the craftsman more and more, yet greater savings by means of industrialisation can be foretold, though in our country they may for the time being still appear Utopian.
   Walter Gropius *letter to the AEG company (1910)*

¶274
Methods based on craftmanship are antiquated and must be replaced by the acceptance of a modern concept of industry. The search for the odd, the wish to be different from one's neighbour, makes unity of style impossible . . . Our age, after a sad interregnum is approaching Zeitstil which will honour traditions but fight false romanticism. Objectivity and reliability are once more gaining ground.
   Walter Gropius *(1910)*

¶275
The need to give one's personal stamp is as important as the inclination to be unobtrusive. In short, it has to do with the need for a personal environment where one can do as one likes; indeed it concerns one of the strongest urges of mankind; the desire for possession.
   . . . To possess something we have to take possession. We have to make it part of ourselves, and it is therefore necessary to reach out for it. To possess something we have to take it in our hand, touch it, test it, put our stamp on it. Something becomes our possession because we make a sign on it, because we give it our name, or defile it, because it shows traces of our existence.
   N J Habraken *'Supports: an Alternative to Mass Housing' (1972)*

¶276

He only moves towards perfection of his art whose criticism surpasses his achievement.

Leonardo da Vinci

¶277

Architecture requires us continually to reinterpret and revalue technology in human and social terms.

Sir Philip Dowson *quoted in 'Contemporary Architects' (1980)*

¶278

If interpretation becomes necessary, architecture may have failed.

Werner Duttmann *quoted in 'Contemporary Architects' (1980)*

¶279

All over Europe the early morning of architecture was spent in the worship of great stones.

W R Lethaby

¶280

Buildings appeal to us in different ways; our eyes may be delighted by the colour, texture and form; our intellect may be stimulated by the skilful use of materials or the brilliance of building technique; or our sense of fitness may be impressed by the excellence of the building for its purpose. In each case, however, we see revealed to us something of the living man, for no architect can give his building a finer quality than exists in his own mind.

Ralph Tubbs *'The Englishman Builds' (1945)*

¶281

Whatever space and time mean, place and occasion mean more. For space in the image of man is place, and time in the image of man is occasion . . . Provide that place, articulate the in between . . . make a welcome of each door and a countenance of each window . . . get closer to the shifting centre of human reality and build its counterform — for each man and all men . . .

Aldo Van Eyck

¶282

Places remembered and places anticipated dovetail in the temporal span of the present. They constitute the real perspective of space.

Aldo Van Eyck

¶283

Architecture need do no more than assist man's 'home-coming'. Since I like to identify architecture with whatever it can effect in human terms, I like to think of it as the constructed counterform of perpetual homecoming. When I speak of house or city as a bunch of places, I imply that you cannot leave a real place without entering another, if it is a real 'bunch'. Departure must mean entry.

Aldo Van Eyck

¶284

A practical architect might not unnaturally conceive the idea of erecting a vast edifice whose frame should be entirely of iron . . . preserving (the frame) by means of a casing of stone.

Eugène-Emmanuel Viollet-le-Duc *'Lectures on Architecture', Vol II (c.1870)*

¶285

More and more people want to determine their own parameters of behaviour. They want to decide how they shall behave, whether it's playing, working, loving, etc. People are less and less prepared to accept imposed rules and patterns of behaviour. Doing your own thing is important.

People are becoming more interested in people and reality, rather than in feeding mythical systems. Unfortunately, however, in terms of doing your own thing, architecture is clearly not working.

Michael Webb and **David Green**

¶286

What we're all looking for is someone who doesn't live there, just pays for it.

Andy Warhol *'From A to B and Back Again' (1975)*

¶287

To be good, according to the vulgar standard of goodness, is obviously quite easy. It merely requires a certain amount of sordid terror, a certain lack of imaginative thought, and a certain low passion for middle-class respectability.

Oscar Wilde *'The Critic as Artist' (1890)*

¶288

If architecture does not serve society it does not serve anything.

Barbara Ward *'The Home of Man'*

¶289

Architects inflict sensory deprivation on their victims through the 'whiteness and lightness and leanness and cleanness and bareness and spareness' of their architecture.

Tom Wolfe *'From Bauhaus to Our House'*

¶290

Buildings should be good neighbours.

Paul Thiry *quoted in 'Contemporary Architects' (1980)*

¶291

The absence of a presence is where it's gone. And the presence of an absence is where it's going.

Peter Eisenman

¶292

We have discovered so many things but not quite what it is in buildings that gives joy.

Ulrik Plesner

¶293

Love architecture for its silence, in which lies its voice.

Gio Ponti

¶294

Measure, guidelines and grids lead to space-time quantities; rhythm, structure and form lead to space-time qualities.

Ulrich Conrads

¶295

Materialistic space transcends itself into sacred space when it becomes a sanctuary for the soul.

Richard England

¶296

Architecture needs a territory to find motivation for its existence, and a territory needs architecture to be qualified as man's environment.

Mario Botta

¶297

From the sound of stone comes the silence of space.

Richard England

¶298

To understand a place one must know its memories.

Richard England

Practice

¶299
Gold medals won't keep the rain out.
A Roderick Males *on technology*

¶300
Most modern buildings hate people.
Professor Joseph Rykwert

¶301
When we are old will we look back and wonder why we did it?
Sam Webb *in 'Architectural Design' (March 1979)*

¶302
Sir, I read in the Press that the set for the BBC's new soap opera East Enders has
been designed to last for 15 years. How many of the tower, deck entry and other
blocks of modern flats built in the real life East End in recent years can be said
to have the same life span, at least in the sense of providing satisfaction to their
inhabitants? We may truly be said to live in a television age when what we see on
the screen has more durability than the reality it portrays.
Yours faithfully,
Christopher Tugendhat *in a letter to 'The Times' (18 February 1985)*

¶303
Madam, you will take what we give you . . .
Louis Sullivan

¶304

Have you boys ever designed a concert hall before?

Frank Lloyd Wright *to Robert Matthew and Leslie Martin while they were designing the Festival Hall*

¶305

Right wing three-quarter – good training for an architect. When you get the ball there will be no ***** to pass it to.

Mr Riley, *a builder, giving advice to his son, Christopher, on entering the University of Liverpool School of Architecture as a student (1947)*

¶306

Oh it's easy lad – if it's new work I ADD; if it's alterations I MULTIPLY.

Mr Riley, *a builder, giving advice to his son, Christopher, on pricing work (1947)*

¶307

Drawing is a way of reasoning on paper.

Saul Steinberg

¶308

A working drawing is merely a letter to a builder telling him precisely what is required of him and not a picture to charm an idiotic client.

Sir Edwin Lutyens

¶309

Core! Those electrics don't 'arf come in thin pipes!

Church hall cleaner, *Cambridge*

¶310

Genius is one per cent inspiration and ninety-nine per cent perspiration.

Thomas Alva Edison *(1896)*

¶311

The first principle of architecture is to get the job.

Henry Richardson

¶312

There are three principles in architecture: get the work, get the work and get the work.

Louis Hellman

¶313

Earth hath not anything to show more fair-faced concrete.

Louis Hellman *revised 'Ode on Westminster Bridge' by Wordsworth*

¶314

Don't count your details before they're hatched.

Louis Hellman

¶315

A lot of water's passed under the cold bridge since then.

Louis Hellman

¶316

The other side of the quoin.

Louis Hellman

¶317

The pope had received many nominations against the architect: that he had cheated, that he had lied, that he had blundered in the construction, that he had spent more than 50,000 ducats when his estimate had been 18,000. The law of Ephesians, according to Vitruvius, would have obliged him to make up the difference. He was a Florentine named Bernardo, hateful to the Sienese from his mere nationality. In his absence, everyone abused him. Pious, when he had inspected the work and examined everything, sent for the man. When he arrived after a few days in some apprehension since he knew that many charges had been brought against him, Pious said, 'You did well, Bernardo, in lying to us about the expense involved in the work. If you had told the truth, you could never have induced us to spend so much money and neither this splendid palace nor this church, the finest in all Italy, would now be standing. Your deceit has built these glorious structures which are praised by all except by a few who are consumed by envy. We thank you and think you deserve a special honour among all architects of our time,' and he ordered full pay to be given him and, in addition, a present of 100 ducats and a scarlet robe.'

Aneas Sylvius, Piccolimini Pious II *Memoirs of a Renaissance Pope*

¶318

Amid a multitude of projects, no plan is devised.

Pulilius Syrus *'Moral Sayings'*

¶319

Most architects in practice today began their professional lives during the high tide of the Modern Movement. For 30 years after 1945 the voice of tradition was stilled and the task of the professional was to build a new world from top to bottom by means – and according to theories – of their own devising. In the 150 years of architecture now the subject of celebration, only one such era occurred. It was the time when schools, hospitals, houses, cathedrals, churches, and public buildings were erected in quantities that today already seem unimaginable. It came about for the sober reason that between 1914 and 1950 the country was at war for the equivalent of one day out of every three-and-a-half.

The Architects' Journal *leading article 'Annus mirabilis 1984' (9 May 1984)*

¶320

The hole that remains when you remove your hands from a bowl of water is the measure of how you will be missed when you leave your job.

Anon

¶321

The bitterness of poor quality is remembered long after the sweetness of the cheapest price is forgotten.

Anon

¶322

... he (Vincent Harris) would start drawing out at the top left-hand corner of the sheet and proceed to complete a plan or elevation to the smallest detail knowing precisely what it would look like when it was built.

Arthur Bailey *in an obituary in 'The Times' (12 August 1971)*

¶323

'I do not want to influence Mr Rushworth,' he continued: 'but, had I a place to new-fashion, I should not put myself into the hands of an improver. I would rather have an inferior degree of beauty, of my own choice, and acquired progressively. I would rather abide by my own blunders than by his.'

Jane Austen *'Mansfield Park' (1814)*

¶324

It is not because things seem difficult that we don't dare. It is because we don't dare that things seem difficult.

Seneca

¶325

It is not generally appreciated that the prime determinants of the built environment are not in any sense architectural. Economic, political, commercial and social factors control most of the major design decisions to such an extent that the actual designer has, all too often, to devote his ingenuity to making the best of a bad job, finding a way to bend the rules to create something which is remotely humane. An obvious example of this is the Housing Cost Yardstick, a bureaucratic cost control tool which has been inflated into the principal determinant in public sector housing. The whole economic and fiscal context in which he works forces the architect to cut initial capital costs at the expense of future cost in use.

Royal Institute of British Architects *evidence given to the UN conference on the Human Environment (June 1972)*

¶326

For which of you, intending to build a tower, sitteth not down first and counteth the cost, whether he have sufficient to finish it?

Luke 14: 28

¶327

These are shrouded in the mists of time, being mentioned by Chaucer and recorded during the building of York Minster. Originally a branch of yew tree would be placed at the highest point of the building to drive away bad spirits. At one time human sacrifice was part of the celebration – in the case of the Cathedral of St Basil in Moscow, the architect was the living sacrifice!! In other cases the architect was deprived of his eyesight as the person best qualified to undertake the role of the guardian spirit of his own creation. Subsequently it was more usual for animals to be used.

Today, topping out is a celebration related to finishing the roofing – making the building weathertight, and is a symbol of the building owners' (and the builders') relief and thankfulness at having got that far in the dangerous and uncertain business of building.

Drink is enjoyed by all, particularly the workmen, suitably amused by the antics of the many strangers to the building site, not seen before, or possibly again.

Owen Luder *on the origins of topping out ceremonies (1984)*

¶328

Whenever you propose to do anything, you should stop and ask yourself – 'If everyone did this, what would the world be like?' You will soon discover the right answer.

Nicholas Monsarrat

¶329

Despite an almost complete lack of formal qualifications, Addison Mizner sprang to wealth and fame as the chief architect employed by those who bought land in Florida during the great property boom. The rich and celebrated scrambled for the cachet of a Mizner-designed residence, despite certain structural drawbacks (engrossed in aesthetic considerations, Mizner once forgot to install a stairway between the first and second stories).

When client William Gray Warden asked for a copy of the blueprints of his Palm Beach house in order to show his friends, Mizner remonstrated, 'Why, the house isn't built yet! Construction first, blueprints afterward.'

(Thus the King of Hearts in Alice's Adventures in Wonderland: 'Sentence first, verdict afterwards.')

Addison Mizner

¶330

It is better to be the architect of a victory than the engineer of a defeat.

Dr John Parker *Urban Design Concept Team – Baltimore (1967)*

¶331

Perhaps the best way to sum up the importance of communication in project management is to quote the highest authority of all – God, who caused the builders of the Tower of Babel to speak many tongues and thus spread confusion and disaster to their project.

Dr John Parker *Oxford Centre for Management Studies – GLC Senior Managers Course*

¶332
Never invest your money in anything that eats or needs repainting.
Billy Rose *millionaire entertainment producer*

¶333
Catch the accidents and convert them into science.
Auguste Rodin

¶334
Thank you for your letter . . . the tenant landlord, Mr Worthington, complained that his dog was able to escape by squeezing under the fence. I explained politely that the fence had been erected in accordance with your drawing and demonstrated that, with the post spacing specified, the slope of the yard is such that a horizontal rail which touches the ground at one end is necessarily some 7″ above the finished surface at the other.

He appeared dissatisfied with this explanation and continued to blame me for the bitch's pregnancy. Without becoming ill-tempered, I pointed out that the animal would soon be too fat to struggle through the gap but that a long term solution would be to acquire a larger dog, such as a St Bernard.

I further proposed that the fence should have been higher, as it appeared that his attractive lady-wife had also strayed during one of his frequent lengthy absences from the premises. At the same time, I asked for an assurance that I would not similarly be held accountable for her condition.
. . . etc etc,
Yours faithfully
R M Renshaw *letter from a contractor to the architect of alterations to a public house*

¶335
Develop an infallible technique and then place yourself at the mercy of inspiration.
Ralph Rapson *quoted in 'Contemporary Architects' (1980)*

¶336
No one sweeps a common hall.
Chinese Proverb

¶337
It is easier to build two chimneys than to maintain one.
English Proverb

¶338
With aching hands and bleeding feet
We dig and heap, lay stone on stone;
We bear the burden and the heat
Of the long day, and wish 'twere done.
Not till the hours of light return,
All we have built do we discern.
Matthew Arnold *'Morality'*

¶339

For over 100 years there was one class of professional men who were thought to be immune from suit. [Architects] were held to owe no duty of care to anyone; because they were quasi-arbitrators . . . If an architect gave a certificate for payment negligently – he could not be sued by either party . . . these decisions were considered by the Court of Appeal . . . The majority of the court felt bound to give immunity to those professional men. But I dissented. Later the House of Lords took the same view . . .

Lord Denning *'The Discipline of the Law'*

¶340

A camel looks like a horse that was planned by a committee.

Vogue *(1958)*

¶341

You'll find in no park or city
A monument to a committee.

Victoria Pasternak

¶342

The appointment of the unfit and the unwilling to do the unnecessary.

Sir David Davenport-Handley *on committees*

¶343

Committee: a group that keeps minutes but squanders hours.

Anon

¶344

A group of men who individually can do nothing but as a group decide that nothing can be done.

Fred Allan *on committees*

¶345

Activity will correspond to opportunity. No client, no building, no building, no architecture. Repeat orders are better.

Professor Sir George Grenfell-Baines *'Thoughts occurring during 50 years in practice'* *(1986)*

¶346

When the meek inherit even a modicum of the earth they are no longer meek.

Professor Sir George Grenfell-Baines *'Thoughts occurring during 50 years in practice'* *(1986)*

¶347

Making a mistake puts one in another position. Capitalise on your catastrophies.

Professor Sir George Grenfell-Baines *'Thoughts occurring during 50 years in practice'* *(1986)*

¶348
Building technology is a science, but the practice of it is an art.
   A Roderick Males

¶349
Don't ask the doctor; ask the patient,
Don't trust the critic; but believe the owner.
   A Roderick Males *on consultancy*

¶350
If you don't know what the client wants, it's your fault.
If the client doesn't know what is offered, it's your fault.
Why? Because he pays the fees.
   A Roderick Males *on the brief*

¶351
The contractor only gives what you ask for, if you don't ask you won't get it.
   A Roderick Males *on tendering*

¶352
Others may comment but it's your name on the certificate.
   A Roderick Males *on liability*

¶353
The client may not hear what you say, but the files will talk in court.
   A Roderick Males *on liability*

¶354
The client may not always see what the architect shows, but always finds the things that are hidden.
   A Roderick Males *on liability*

¶355
Tell the client, she may be cross today, but if you don't she'll sue tomorrow.
   A Roderick Males *on liability*

¶356
What you know matters,
Who you know matters,
Who knows what you know matters even more.
   A Roderick Males *on success*

¶357
The song of the receiver: what is not nailed down is mine.
Whatever I can prise loose is not nailed down.
   A Roderick Males *on receivership*

¶358

He [Sir Edwin Lutyens] had been commissioned by Lloyd George, only two weeks before it was needed, to design a catafalque past which the troops could march in the victory parade of 1919. He quickly sketched the design for his temporary monument. It was built in wood and plaster and was an instant success. Next day *The Times* in a leading article demanded that it be rebuilt in stone and by November 11 1920 the body of the Unknown Warrior was carried past Lutyens' new stone cenotaph.

Roderick Gradidge *in 'The Times' (14 November 1981)*

¶359

Building defects soon cease to be a growth industry when the builder becomes the landlord, if only temporarily.

Ken Dixon *'Economics of State Housing in the UK' (1982)*

¶360

Those who would carry out the great public schemes must be proof against the most fatiguing delays, the most mortifying disappointments, the most shocking insults and, most of all, the presumptions, judgements of the ignorant upon their designs.

Edmund Burke

Craven Images

¶361

To the average man or woman . . . these figures will be occasions . . . for vulgarity and of unwholesome talk, calculated to lead to practices of which there are more than enough in the purlieus of the Strand already . . . they are a form of statuary which no careful father would wish his daughter to see . . . For a certain type of mind, on the other hand, it cannot but have a demoralizing tendency.

Father Vaughan *on Epstein's 'Strand Statues' quoted in the 'Evening Standard'*

¶362

Travel up to Northampton and see the statue of the madonna and child in this church. My horses may be all wrong; we may all be wrong; but I'm damned sure that isn't right.

Sir Alfred Manning *on the work of Henry Moore*

¶363

Sculptor Henry Moore has been asked not to leave any holes in which boys could trap their heads when he carves 'Family Group' for Harlow New Town.

News Chronicle

¶364

The statues are hideous beyond words, they seem to be a sort of primitive caveman production, and unworthy of a good place on any public building in London.

Morning Post *on the work of Henry Moore (April 1929)*

¶365

I took my children to see some of Henry Moore's chunky abstract sculptures in Hyde Park. My daughter Laura, 7, said, 'Look, something's fallen off a jumbo jet'.
Spike Milligan

¶366

Sculpture: Mud pies which endure.
Cyril Connolly

¶367

In support of his plea for a greater use of brickwork carving, Ritchie suggests that space should be found on projects for apprentice craftsmen to try their hands at a skill, which he claims is not difficult. 'We might have' he says 'portraits of the architect, Raquel Welch and the general foreman in an unexpected corner of the building! God knows that is what some of our buildings need – humour and humanity.' The architect presumably provides the humour, the general foreman provides the humanity, but where on earth does Miss Raquel Welch fit into Mr Ritchie's scheme of things?
Walter Ritchie *quoted by Kate Wharton, in 'The Architect' (December 1973)*

¶368

. . . s/he might feel impelled to comment on the history of the building, perhaps as a border to the name panel.

Every building has a saga the public rarely suspects and while the construction industry includes men of courage, energy and resource, the message for posterity may run –
THIS BUILDING WAS COMPLETED IN JUNE 1974 DESPITE TWO STRIKES – VANDALISM – FRED FRACTURING HIS HIP – VAT – AND SAMANTHA WIFE OF THE GENERAL FOREMAN . . .
Walter Ritchie *'Sign Your Name with Pride', in 'Building' (30 August 1974)*

¶369

Cornice or frieze with bossy sculpture graven.
John Milton *'Paradise Lost', Bk i, l 715*

¶370

The turd in the plaza.
James Wines, *SITE Inc., referring to modern works of sculpture placed outside banal modern office blocks*

The Critics

¶371

Critics always want to put you into pigeon holes, which can be very uncomfortable unless you happen to be a pigeon.

Max Adrian *quoted by Barry Norman in 'The Times' (4 July 1972)*

¶372

Pleasure is by no means an infallible critical guide, but it is the least fallible.

W H Auden *'The Dyer's Hand (1962)*

¶373

The relationship between architects and the media is based on trust and understanding. The architects don't trust the media and the media don't understand the architects.

Scorpio *columnist in 'Building Design' (29 August 1986)*

¶374

What of the Architectural Correspondent?
If he gets it wrong, he gets ignored, ridiculed and occasionally sued for libel – on which note I think I have said quite enough.

Nicholas Tomalin *'Two Cheers'*

¶375

Wallis Gilbert & Partners' (architects of the Hoover Factory etc) work was generally criticised by *AR* and it is said that one of the partners arrived at Queen Anne's Gate with a horsewhip but failed to find the editor in.

Sir John Betjeman *in 'Architectural Review' (October 1973)*

¶376

On how many newspaper staffs shall we find, besides the dramatic, literary and musical critics, an architectural critic? With how many casual dinner-party neighbours should we dare to substitute the latest London building for the latest London play as a feeler topic? How many schools have on their staffs an architectural master?

Sir Clough and Lady Amabel Williams-Ellis *'The Pleasures of Architecture' (1924)*

¶377

The self-appointed 'gentlemen' of the press, these senile young men and aged adolescents, best-preserved preservationists, conservationists, antiquarianists and retrogrades of all sorts, grounded in reaction, drug us into the morass of induced nostalgia, ignoring the rhythm of today. But fetishism of the past is in reality but a lack of confidence of the future, and a fear of rupture with the safely familiar. These arbiters of trivial values, the fake quasi-neo's, dream of a mass return to a distant gas-lit womb. No, I fear architects will search in vain for enlightenment or inspiration from that quarter.

Berthold Lubetkin *RIBA President's invitation lecture (1985)*

¶378

A critic is a bundle of biases held loosely together by a sense of taste.

Whitney Balliett *'Dinosaurs in the Morning' (1926)*

¶379

Too many scribes in the temple; too much 'in talk'; too much writing with a nudge or a wink to the knowing – these contemporary diseases common to all the arts are ultimately degrading and rightly rejected by the public.

Sir Hugh Casson *in an essay on journalism*

¶380

Criticism of the arts in London, taken by and large, ends in a display of suburban omniscience which sees no further than the next door garden.

Sir Thomas Beecham *quoted by Neville Cardus in 'Sir Thomas Beecham'*

¶381

Critics are like eunuchs in a harem: they know how it's done, they've seen it done every day, but they're unable to do it themselves.

Brendan Behan

Mother of the Arts

¶382
The British believe that beauty is unmanly and should be left to foreigners and women.

Sir Hugh Casson

¶383
To have an avant-garde you have to have a garde.

Sir Hugh Casson *quoted in 'The Daily Telegraph' (13 January 1984)*

¶384
'There is a huge surge of interest in the quality of the environment. Art is a vital ingredient in keeping the quality of life going', Sir Hugh Casson, an architect and former president of the Royal Academy, told Westminster Chamber of Commerce in April 1985.

But he attributed the lack of ornament on so many twentieth-century buildings to fear. It was not due to lack of funds: 'It is all part of the British war against the senses. The British always believe that art is a very wet exercise done by wet people on wet afternoons'.

Sir Hugh Casson *quoted in 'Environmental Education'*

¶385
In my experience, if you have to keep the lavatory door shut by extending your left leg, it's modern architecture.

Nancy Banks Smith *in 'The Guardian' (1969)*

¶386

Architecture aims at Eternity; and therefore is the only thing incapable of modes and fashions in its principles.

Sir Christopher Wren *'Parentalia'*

¶387

A nation which lives a pastoral and innocent life never decorates the shepherd's staff or the plough handle; but races who live by depredation and slaughter nearly always bestow exquisite ornaments on the quiver, the helmet and the spear.

John Ruskin *'The Two Paths' (1859)*

¶388

I am all for ornament; my heart beats for scrambled egg on the walls. But I don't believe in ornament that results from buying history by the foot. I believe in inventing ornament where it is intrinsic to the structure of the thing made.

Emilio Ambasz

¶389

Ornamentation is the principal part of architecture, considered as a subject of fine art.

John Ruskin *'True and Beautiful: Sculpture'*

¶390

We make buildings for our need, and then, sacrificing our pockets to art, cover them with a mass of purely nonsensical forms which we hope may turn them into fine architecture.

Roger Fry *in a letter to 'The Times' (1912)*

¶391

The world is still deceived with ornament.

William Shakespeare *'The Merchant of Venice' Act III, Scene ii*

¶392

Not only is ornament produced by criminals but also a crime is committed through the fact that ornament inflicts serious injury on people's health, on the national budget and hence on cultural evolution.

Adolf Loos *'Ornament and Crime' (1908)*

¶393

Trying to learn architecture in a school is like trying to learn about love from a sex manual.

Louis Hellman

¶394

Art is not a special sauce applied to ordinary cooking; it is the cooking itself if it is good.

W R Lethaby *'Form in Civilisation'*

¶395

Artists are not engineers of the soul.

John F Kennedy *in a speech at the dedication of the Robert Frost Laboratory (November 1962)*

¶396

Every master knows that the material teaches the artist.

Ilya Ehrenburg *in 'Saturday Review' (30 September 1967)*

¶397

I imagined asking her whether she liked Le Corbusier, and her replying, 'Love some, with a little Benedictine if you've got it'.

Peter de Vries *'Tunnel of Love' (1954)*

¶398

In other countries art and literature are left to a lot of shabby bums living in attics and feeding on booze and spaghetti, but in America the successful writer or picture painter is indistinguishable from any other decent businessman.

Sinclair Lewis *'Babbitt' (1922)*

¶399

A work of art is no good if it doesn't provoke a furore.

Sir Isiah Berlin *in 'The Observer' (2 November 1980)*

¶400

I wanted to become a work of art myself, and not an artist.

Bernard Berenson *'Sunset and Twilight', in 'Diaries 1947-58'*

¶401

The lower one's vitality, the more sensitive one is to great art.

Max Beerbohm *'Seven Men' (1919)*

¶402

Art is born of humiliation.

W H Auden *quoted by Humphrey Carpenter in 'Auden: A Biography'*

¶403

No architecture is so haughty as that which is simple.

John Ruskin *'The Stones of Venice' (1851–53)*

¶404

It is useful because it is beautiful.

Antoine de Saint-Exupéry

¶405

I believe that architects should design gardens to be used, as much as the houses they build, to develop a sense of beauty and the taste and inclination toward the fine arts and other spiritual values.

Luis Barragán

¶406

The soul needs more space than the body.

Axel Munthe

¶407

The art of architecture studies not structure in itself but the effect of structure on the human spirit.

Geoffrey Scott

¶408

But early in the nineteenth century . . . architecture was removed from the sphere of everyday life and placed under the jealous guardianship of experts and aesthetes. Faith became a substitute for knowledge and very soon the ordinary person came to consider architecture in the same light as higher mathematics or Hegelian philosophy; as something which he could never hope properly to understand and possessed of a scale of values that he must take on trust.

Sir Osbert Lancaster *'Pillar to Post' (1938)*

¶409

What distinguishes modern architecture is surely a new sense of space and the machine aesthetic.

Alan Colquhoun

¶410

Here it must be enough to state that what is most disastrous in the visual arts of the twentieth century and what is most hopeful was fully in existence by the time the Age of the World Wars dawned.

Sir Nikolaus Pevsner *'The Sources of Modern Architecture and Design' (1968)*

¶411

There should be no features about a building which are not necessary for convenience, construction or propriety . . . the smallest detail should . . . serve a purpose, and construction itself should vary with the material employed.

Augustus W N Pugin *'The True Principles of Pointed or Christian Architecture' (1841)*

¶412

Architecture and design for the masses must be functional, in the sense that they must be acceptable to all and that their well-functioning is the primary necessity.

Sir Nikolaus Pevsner *'The Sources of Modern Architecture and Design' (1968)*

¶413

The challenge for the modern architect is the same as the challenge for all of us in our lives: to make out of the ordinary something out-of-the-ordinary.

Dr Patrick Nuttgens *'Architecture for Everyman', the BBC Television Programme, and reprinted in 'The Listener' (1 March 1979)*

¶414

There are three arts – painting, music and ornamental pastry making; of which last architecture is a sub-division.

Pastry cook *quoted in F and V Meynell's 'The Week-End Book'*

¶415

I don't think one 'comes down' from Jimmy's university. According to him, it's not even red brick, but white tile.

John Osborne *'Look Back in Anger' II i*

¶416

Post-Modernism has become a pep-pill to make even the most timid of architects brave . . . a refuge for people who cannot design.

Sumet Jumsai

¶417

I must study politics and war that my sons may have liberty to study mathematics and philosophy. My sons ought to study mathematics and philosophy, geography, natural history, naval architecture, navigation, commerce, and agriculture, in order to give their children a right to study painting, poetry, music, architecture, statuary, tapestry, and porcelain.

John Adams *in a letter to Abigail Adams*

¶418

Shall we attempt to condense the central issue facing architecture today into one sentence?
Colours which you can see with ears; sounds to see with eyes; the void you touch with your elbows; the taste of space on your tongue; the fragrance of dimensions; the juice of stone.

Marcel Breuer *quoted in 'Contemporary Architects' (1980)*

¶419

In attitudes of acute discomfort nymphs and tribal deities of excessive female physique and alarming size balanced precariously on broken pediments, threatening the passer-by with a shower of stone fruit from the cavernous interiors of their inevitable cornucopia.

Sir Osbert Lancaster *'Edwardian Baroque', in 'Pillar to Post' (1938)*

¶420

A hundred and fifty accurate reproductions of Anne Hathaway's cottage, each complete with central heating and garage.

Sir Osbert Lancaster *'Stockbrokers Tudor', in 'Pillar to Post' (1938)*

¶421

The resulting style, known as Bankers Georgian, always preserves something of the air of a Metro-Goldwyn-Mayer production of 'The School for Scandal'.

Sir Osbert Lancaster *'Bankers Georgian' in 'Pillar to Post' (1938)*

¶422

Architectural Association (or Beggar's Opera) Georgian . . . may be distinguished by its invincible refinement.

Sir Osbert Lancaster *'Bankers Georgian', in 'Pillar to Post' (1938)*

¶423

The capacity of historical architecture to employ our perception and imagination for a long time establishes a psychological connexion between us and our environment, the latter being experienced as 'interesting'. In comparison, average modern architecture offers remarkably little visual information. Neither does the modern repertoire contain any symbolic aspect nor any considerable amount of 'aesthetic information'. Working to a general grid pattern the new architecture explores the principle of endless addition and repetition of a few elemental norms: once we have seen the corner we have seen the whole. Normally the effect is monotony and our reaction boredom, if significance is not achieved by unusual height or outline.

Theo Crosby *'How to Play the Environment Game' (1973)*

¶424

We must recreate the classicality of the spirit – classical education rather than classical derivation.

Gio Ponti

¶425

Why did the modern movement keep reminding us that Cathedrals were once white but never that Greek temples were multi-coloured?

Richard England

¶426

In matters of grave importance, style, not sincerity, is the vital thing.

Oscar Wilde *'The Importance of Being Earnest'*

¶427

Great art embodies a high sense of play.

Herbert Whone *'The Hidden Face of Music'*

¶428

I don't want realism, I want magic.

Tennessee Williams

¶429

An enterprise to improve the style of cottage architecture! When you have got my ornaments ready, I will wear them.

Henry David Thoreau *'Walden or, Life in the Woods'*

¶430

A great proportion of architectural ornaments are literally hollow, and a September gale would strip them off, like borrowed plumes, without injury to the substantials.

Henry David Thoreau *'Walden or, Life in the Woods'*

¶431

All work passes out of the hands of the architect into the hands of nature, to be perfected.

Henry David Thoreau

¶432

What reasonable man ever supposed that ornaments were something outward and in the skin merely, – that the tortoise got his spotted shell, or the shell-fish its mother-o'-pearl tints, by such a contract as the inhabitants of Broadway their Trinity Church?

Henry David Thoreau *'Walden or, Life in the Woods'*

¶433

True, there are architects so called in this country, and I have heard of one at least possessed with the idea of making architectural ornaments have a core of truth, a necessity, and hence a beauty, as if it were a revelation to him. All very well perhaps from his point of view, but only a little better than the common dilettantism.

Henry David Thoreau *'Walden or, Life in the Woods'*

¶434

The artist is not a special kind of man. Every man is a special kind of artist.

Eric Gill

¶435

A sham gothic building I was shown over contained in its entrance hall a new electric switchboard. In reply to the question how I liked the building, I said I liked the switchboard. My friend, a scientist said he thought that was just the kind of thing I would not like – I said 'Oh I like anything reasonable'.

Eric Gill

¶436

A student at the Massachusetts Institute of Technology once asked Fuller whether he took aesthetic factors into account when tackling a technical problem. 'No,' replied Fuller, 'When I am working on a problem, I never think about beauty. I think only of how to solve the problem. But when I have finished, if the solution is not beautiful, I know it is wrong.'

R Buckminster Fuller

¶437

For though he builds glorious temples, 'tis odd
He leaves never a doorway to get in a God.

James Russell Lowell *'A Fable for Critics'*

¶438

Life is very nice, but it lacks form. It's the aim of art to give it some.

Jean Anouilh 'The Rehearsal' (1960)

¶439

Simple was its noble architecture. Each ornament arrested, as it were, in its position, seemed to have been placed there of necessity.

François-Marie Arouet Voltaire 'Le Temple du Goût'

¶440

. . . the artist has an imperative need to make others share the joy which he experiences himself.

Igor Stravinsky 'An Autobiography' (1936)

¶441

People spend so much of their time on holiday and at weekends going to see buildings of the past because they are a pleasure. You don't get people going to look at modern buildings as part of a pleasure concern; they go to look at old buildings because they are fun. They don't go and look at the square slab blocks of the 1930s, but they do go to the Chrysler Building, the Empire State Building and the Rockefeller Center which are decorative modern buildings.

Terry Farrell (1985)

¶442

A more expressive technology is very much part of an architecture which follows on after modernism . . . The European tradition, particularly of Arts and Crafts and Art Nouveau, took so much of its inspiration from how things were made; the studded wall-cladding of Otto Wagner, the elaborate but prefabricated cast-iron elements of Hector Guimard's metro stations and the sculptured r.s.j.'s of C R Mackintosh were all outstanding combinations of art and technology.

Terry Farrell (1984)

¶443

Immature artists imitate, mature artists steal.

Lionel Trilling in 'Esquire' (1962)

¶444

In any civilisation the mannered imitation of the past, of a mock historical kind, usually means impending collapse.

Arnold Toynbee

¶445

Sight is one of man's great gifts. To have eyes that do not see but merely record, is to be dead to at least one aspect of the world. Whether architecture is to deteriorate into a crude commercialism, whether it is to be devitalized by subservience to architectural clichés, or whether it is to become one of the finest means of expression of mankind, will largely depend on a new visual awareness. Without this, architecture is but music to the deaf.

Ralph Tubbs 'The Englishman Builds' (1945)

¶446

Historical periods don't die they are just reinterpreted.
  Charles Gwathmey

¶447

The Gothic cathedral is a blossoming in stone subdued by the insatiable demand of harmony in man. The mountain of granite blooms into an eternal flower.
  Ralph Waldo Emerson *'Essays, First Series: History'*

¶448

Beauty is successful expression.
  Benedetto Croce

¶449

Art is the expression of the profoundest thought in the simplest way.
  Albert Einstein

¶450

Art, the creative process, is the solution of problems that cannot be formulated clearly, before they have been solved.
  Piet Hein

¶451

Art is as important as council housing.
  Illtyd Harrington (1975)

¶452

Undecided as to whether a thousand gallon water-tank looked better disguised as the baptistry at Pisa or was more discreetly housed in a tactful reinterpretation of the Petit Trianon.
  Sir Osbert Lancaster *on the Coca-Colonial Style*

¶453

A style of Architecture [the Gothic] which, to me at least is, in comparison with all others, the most beautiful of all, and by far the most in harmony with the mysteries of religion.
  John Keble *'Lectures on Poetry No. 3'*

¶454

It is very good advice to believe only what an artist does, rather than what he says about his work.
  David Hockney (1976)

¶455

A true artist takes no notice whatever of the public. The public to him are non-existent. He leaves that to the popular novelist.
  Oscar Wilde *'The Soul of Man under Socialism' (1891)*

¶456

The moment you cheat for the sake of beauty, you know you are an artist.

Max Jacob *'Art poétique' (1922)*

¶457

Gnomes always draw curtains where there are views.

Ada Louise Huxtable *in 'The New York Times' (16 November 1975)*

¶458

Artists are the unacknowledged legislators of the world.

Dr Jonathan Miller (1964)

¶459

The building which is fitted accurately to its end will turn out to be beautiful, though beauty is not intended.

Georg Moller *'Essays on Architecture'*

¶460

We all see more of architecture than of any other art. Every street is a gallery of architects' work, and in most streets, whatever their age, there is good work and bad. Through these amusing shows many of us walk unperceivingly all our days, like illiterates in a library, so richly does the fashionable education provide us with blind sides.

C E Montague *'The Right Place'*

¶461

The human pleasures of life are what I mean by art.

William Morris

¶462

Meanwhile if these hours are dark do not let us sit deedless like fools and fine gentlemen. Rather let us put our workshop in order against that great day when there is an art made by the people and for the people as a joy for the maker and the user.

William Morris *'The Arts of the People'*

¶463

A work of art has no importance whatever to society. It is only important to the individual.

Vladimir Nabokov *'Strong Opinions' (1974)*

¶464

The real lesson for British architects from American Post-Modern Classicism is that the British are too precious and over-stuffy in their concerns. If British modernism's failure was that it took itself too earnestly, too joyously and seriously, it seems inevitable that establishment modern architects prefer Quinlan Terry's 'properly done' classicism to anything freewheeling and interpretive like Venturi, Stern or Graves. The puritanical zeal underlying the reaction of establishment Britain to the frothy sensuality of Post-Modern Classicism was expressed well be Quinlan Terry who called it 'The Work of Satan'.

Terry Farrell (1985)

¶465
Imagination – it is that deceitful part in man, that mistress of error and falsity . . .

Pascal *'Pensées' (1670)*

¶466
In the greenest of our valleys
By good angels tenanted,
Once a fair and stately palace
(Radiant palace) reared its head.
In the monarch Thought's dominion
It stood there!
Never seraph spread a pinion
Over fabric half so fair.

Edgar Allan Poe *'The Haunted Palace', in 'The Fall of the House of Usher'*

¶467
Poets and painters abstain from celebrating the White House or Buckingham Palace, buildings of no mean importance in the life of the nations but low on spiritual assets. At best they figure on postage stamps, but no artist worth his salt wants to have anything to do with them.

Bernard Rudofsky *'The Prodigious Builders' (1977)*

¶468
You know there are a great many odd styles of architecture about; you don't want to do anything ridiculous; you hear of me, among others, as a respectable architectural man-milliner; and you send for me, that I may tell you the leading fashion.

John Ruskin *'The Crown of Wild Olive' (1866)*

¶469
He who resolves never to ransack any mind but his own will be reduced, from mere barrenness, to the poorest of all imitations: he will be obliged to imitate himself.

Sir Joshua Reynolds *speaking to students of the Royal Academy*

¶470
Art never initiates. It merely takes over what is already present in the real world and makes an aesthetic pattern out of it, or tries to explain it, or tries to relate it to some other aspect of life.

Anthony Burgess (1974)

¶471

Always design a thing by considering it in its larger context: a chair in a room, a room in a house, a house in an environment, an environment in a city plan.

Eero Saarinen *quoted in 'Time' (1956)*

¶472

Lovely promise and quick ruin are seen nowhere better than in Gothic architecture.

George Santayana *'Avila, Persons and Places: The Background of My Life' (1944)*

¶473

Away with medievalism, then, and the medieval concept of handicrafts themselves, as mere training and means for the purposes of form.

Oskar Schlemmer *discarding the crafts approach at the Bauhaus (1922)*

¶474

Art is the right hand of nature.

Friedrich von Schiller *'Fiesco' (1783)*

¶475

The artistic temperament is a disease that afflicts amateurs.

G K Chesterton *'Heretics' (1905)*

¶476

If it is art it is not for all and if it is for all it is not art.

Arnold Schoenberg

¶477

Beauty in architecture has to be sought from within a world comprising 'a welter of commercial and municipal monstrosities. It is as though one had to tune a violin in the midst of a railway accident'.

Geoffrey Scott *'The Architecture of Humanism' (1914)*

¶478

The world of sight is still limitless. It is the artist who limits vision to the cramped dimension of his own ego.

Marya Mannes *'More in Anger' (1958)*

¶479

It is dangerous to let the public behind the scenes. They are easily disillusioned and then they are angry with you for it was the illusion they loved.

W Somerset Maugham

¶480

The artist's egotism is outrageous: it must be; he is by nature a solipsist and the world exists only for him to exercise upon it his powers of creation.

W Somerset Maugham *'The Summing Up' (1938)*

¶481

Art is not a mirror to reflect the world, but a hammer with which to shape it.
Vladimir Mayakovsky

¶482

Of all forms of visible otherworldliness, it seems to be, the Gothic is at once the most logical and the most beautiful. It reaches up magnificently – and a good half of it is palpably useless.
H L Mencken *'The New Architecture', in 'The American Mercury' (February 1931)*

¶483

Ugly is only half way to a thing.
George Meredith

¶484

The search for architecture in the empty desert of graphics is but sophism.
Konstantin Melnikov *'Architectural Design'*

¶485

Michelangelo was seventy-two years old when he was appointed chief architect of St Peter's and commissioned to embellish this great temple with his paintings and statues. For eighteen years he continued this work, which made his fame as imperishable as the church itself. Toward the end, when his eyesight failed and he had become feeble, he had his servants carry him into the great halls and galleries and chapels, where he had labored with such vim and enthusiasm. He would run his hands over the statues and carvings, feeling out with his dextrous fingers the details that his eye could no longer see, and he often exclaimed, 'I still learn.'
Michelangelo Buonarroti

¶486

A great work of art is a kind of suicide.
A Alvarez

¶487

Aesthetic value is often the by-product of the artist striving to do something else.
Mark Amory (ed) *'The Letters of Evelyn Waugh' (1980)*

¶488

All changed, changed utterly: A terrible beauty is born.
W B Yeats

¶489

If beauty isn't genius it usually signals at least a high level of animal cunning.
Peter York *in 'London Collection' (1978)*

¶490
Send to us power and light . . .
Harrow the house of the dead; look shining at
New styles of architecture, a change of heart.
   W H Auden 'Petition'

¶491
All art is a kind of confession . . . All artists, if they are to survive, are forced, at last, to tell the whole story, to vomit the anguish up.
   James Baldwin 'Nobody Knows My Name' (1961)

¶492
The simple power of necessity is to a certain degree a principle of beauty; and these structures so plainly manifest this necessity that you feel a strange emotion in contemplating them.
   Paul Bourget 'Outremer' (1895)

¶493
Definition of good design: An object is well designed where the relationship of the part to the part and the part to the whole shall appear to be inevitable.
   Anon

¶494
There is no more sombre enemy of good art than the pram in the hall.
   Cyril Connolly 'Enemies of Promise' (1938)

¶495
More and more, so it seems to me, light is the beautifier of the building.
   Frank Lloyd Wright

¶496
Light, God's eldest daughter, is a principal beauty in a building.
   Thomas Fuller 'Holy State' Bk 1 Ch 3

¶497
In the elder days of Art,
Builders wrought with greatest care
Each minute and unseen part;
For the Gods see everywhere.
   H W Longfellow 'The Builders'

¶498
God sees the back.
   Walter Ritchie

Town, City, Suburb

¶499

Clearly, then, the city is not a concrete jungle, it is a human zoo.

Desmond Morris *'The Human Zoo' (1969)*

¶500

As a remedy to life in society I would suggest the big city. Nowadays it is the only desert within our means.

Albert Camus *'Notebooks' (1935–42)*

¶501

He so improved the city that he justly boasted he had found it brick and left it marble.

Gaius Suetonius *'Augustus 28'*

¶502

Britain, far from being a 'decadent democracy', is a Spartan country. This is mainly due to the British way of building towns, which dispenses with the reasonable comfort enjoyed by all other weak and effeminate peoples of the world . . . in every other country, it has been explained, people just build streets and towns following their own common sense. England is the only country of the world where there is a Ministry of Town and Country planning. That is the real reason for the muddle.

George Mikes *'How to be an Alien' (1946)*

¶503

Arriving at each new city, the traveller finds again a past of his that he did not know he had: the foreignness of what you no longer are or no longer possess lies in wait for you in foreign, unpossessed places.

Italo Calvino *'Invisible Cities' (1974)*

¶504

The people are the city.

William Shakespeare *'Coriolanus'*

¶505

Your weakness, city, is that you have a soul.

Lawrence Hartmus

¶506

The materials of city planning are sky, space, trees, steel and cement in that order and in that hierarchy.

Le Corbusier *quoted in 'The Times' (1965)*

¶507

This much is certain: the town has no room for the citizen – no meaning at all – unless he is gathered into its meaning. As for architecture, it need do no more than assist man's homecoming.

Aldo Van Eyck

¶508

Magna civitas, magna solitudo
A great city, a great loneliness.

Anon

¶509

People coming from the country see lots of houses but they do not see the city.

Agricola

¶510

The hand that signed the paper felled the City.

Dylan Thomas

¶511

'What meaning does your construction have?' he asks. 'What is the aim of a city under construction unless it is a city? Where is the plan you are following, the blueprint?'

'We will show it to you as soon as the working day is over; we cannot interrupt our work now,' they answer.

Work stops at sunset. Darkness falls over the building site. The sky is filled with stars. 'There is the blueprint,' they say.

Italo Calvino *'Invisible Cities' (1974)*

¶512

Cities, like cats, will reveal themselves at night.

Rupert Brooke *'Letters from America'*

¶513

A quiet city is a contradiction in terms. It is a thing uncanny, spectral.

Max Beerbohm *'Advertisements, Mainly On The Air' (1946)*

¶514

A great city is not to be confounded with a populous one.

Aristotle *'Politics'*

¶515

No city should be too large for a man to walk out of it in a morning

Cyril Connolly *'The Unquiet Grave' (1945)*

¶516

Men, not walls, make a city.

Chinese Proverb

¶517

For a city consists in its men, and not in its walls nor ships empty of men.

Nicias

¶518

The great cities of the twentieth century look like something which has burst an intolerable envelope and splashed.

H G Wells *'Anticipations'*

¶519

Architects and city fathers would be surprised at the amount of public concern over a city's skyline.

Ada Louise Huxtable *'Kicked a Building Lately?' (1976)*

¶520

The city's skyline is a physical representation of its facts of life. But a skyline is also a potential work of art.

Paul Spreiregen *'Urban Design' (1965)*

¶521

In colonial days the accents of skylines proclaimed an hierarchy of values. Characteristically, the skyline consisted of church steeples at a high point with a domed building, usually a seat of government, as the focus. Fire watch towers, shot towers, or signal towers had distinct profiles and did not add confusion – neither did a cluster of ships' masts in the harbor, for they were thin, almost lacelike. All of these secondary skyline features had secondary visual roles which complemented the one or two prime skyline accents. Our contemporary skylines cannot be read in such a simple way.

Paul Spreiregen *'Urban Design' (1965)*

¶522
The town is new every day.
Estonian Proverb

¶523
The city should be an organisation of love ... the best economy in cities is the care and culture of men.
Lewis Mumford

¶524
I have an affection for a great city. I feel safe in the neighbourhood of man, and enjoy the sweet security of the streets.
H W Longfellow *'Driftwood' (1857)*

¶525
There is no solitude in the world like that of the big city.
Kathleen Norris

¶526
God made the country, man made the town.
William Cowper *'The Task'*

¶527
God the first garden made, and the first city Cain.
Abraham Cowley *'The Garden'*

¶528
If ever we are to have a time of architecture again, it must be founded on a love for the city. No planting down of a few costly buildings, ruling some straight streets, provision of fountains or setting up of stone, or bronze dolls is enough without the enthusiasm for corporate life and common ceremonial. Every noble city has a crystallization of the contentment, pride and order of the community.
W R Lethaby

¶529
A city that is set on a hill cannot be hid.
Matthew 4:14

¶530
They ain't making it anymore.
Mark Twain *on land*

¶531
Cities are the sinks of the human race.
Jean-Jacques Rousseau *'Emile'*

¶532

When I was a child the streets of any city were full of street vendors and street entertainers of every kind, and of the latter the Italian organ-grinder with his monkey was one of the most endearing. Today, officialdom seems to have banished them all, and the only persons who still earn their living on the streets are prostitutes and dope peddlers.

W H Auden 'A Certain World'

¶533

For students of the troubled heart
Cities are perfect works of art.

Christopher Morley

¶534

One cannot zone a steel rolling mill in the middle of a domestic housing area, but it is wrong to be too clinical in separating the various activities of a community. It tends to create an evening and weekend man, a work man, a shopping man and a recreational man; whereas at one time a community of whole men provided the necessary contact for complete social identity.

The High Wycombe Society, Buckinghamshire *Evidence given to the UN Conference on the Human Environment (June 1972)*

¶535

I am not talking about blueprints or development plans, and all that committee fodder that gathers dust in municipal archives, but more about imagery. Throughout history, from the vision of battlemented white towers on a distant hill as in Renaissance painting, to the glitter and raucous vulgarity of New York's Broadway in the 1930s – 'the city' has been an idea to quicken the pulse and lift the heart; it is a quality of excitement which London on a warm spring evening still abundantly has . . . To retain, or regain their magnetism, cities are going to have to adapt to new economic facts of life in ways we can only dimly perceive at present.

Anne Sofer *in 'The Times' (14 May 1984)*

¶536

Memory of travel is the stuff of our fairest dreams. Splendid cities, plazas, monuments and landscapes that pass before our eyes, and we enjoy again the charming and impressive spectacles that we have formerly experienced.

Camillo Sitte *'The Art of Building Cities' (1945)*

¶537

Oh, blank confusion! true epitome
Of what the mighty city is herself,
To thousands upon thousands of her sons,
Living amid the same perpetual whirl
Of trivial objects, melted and reduced
To one identity, by differences
That have no law, no meaning, and no end –

William Wordsworth *'Prelude' Book VIII*

¶538

Only by returning to life in the city does one rediscover the unbelievable complexity, excitement, and beauty of the human face. There are faces in the country, of course, but they are widely spaced like filling stations.

Jerome Weidman

¶539

The thing generally raised on city land is taxes.

Charles Dudley Warner *'Sixteenth Week', in 'My Summer in a Garden' (1871)*

¶540

Happy is that city which in time of peace thinks of war.

Anon *Inscription in the armoury of Venice*

¶541

In a great town friends are scattered; so that there is not that fellowship, for the most part, which is in less neighbourhoods.

Francis Bacon *'Of Friendship' Essays (1625)*

¶542

The improvement in city conditions by the general adoption of the motor-car can hardly be over-estimated. Streets clean, dustless and odorless, with light rubber-tired vehicles moving swiftly and noiselessly over their smooth expanse, would eliminate a greater part of the nervousness, distraction and strain of modern metropolitan life.

Scientific American

¶543

The car is the greatest problem for architecture.

Walter Gropius *quoted in 'The Sunday Times' (1960)*

¶544

If a large city can, after intense intellectual efforts, choose for its mayor a man who merely will not steal from it, we consider it a truth of the suffrage.

Frank Lloyd Wright

¶545

Architecture is only part of the problem of cities. Conceivably we could have a great city of mediocre buildings. It might be a happy place in which to live. And you might have a beautiful city that is not a happy city.

Allan Temko *'The City'*

¶546

Much hath been done, but more remains to do –
Their galleys blaze – why not their city too?

Lord Byron *'The Corsair'*

¶547

I am convinced that, after the fundamental question of preserving peace, it is the form and organisation of urban areas that is now looming up as the greatest social challenge for the world for the rest of this century.

Colin Buchanan

¶548

Match me such marvel save in Eastern clime,
A rose-red city – 'half as old as Time!'

J W Burgon *'Petra' 132*

¶549

And I saw a new heaven and a new earth: for the first heaven and the first earth were passed away; and there was no more sea. And I John saw the holy city, new Jerusalem, coming down from God out of heaven, prepared as a bride adorned for her husband.

Revelations 21:1

¶550

The street of the city was pure gold.

Revelations 21:21

¶551

Woe to the bloody city! It is all full of lies and robbery; the prey departeth not.

Nahum 3:1

¶552

But Paul said, I am a man which am a Jew of Tarsus, a city in Cilicia, a citizen of no mean city.

Acts 21:39

¶553

The new white cliffs of the City are built in vain.

Sir John Betjeman *'Monody on the Death of Aldersgate Station'*

¶534

A Garden City is a Town designed for healthy living and industry; of a size that makes possible a full measure of social life but not larger; surrounded by a rural belt; the whole of the land being in public ownership or held in trust for the community.

Garden Cities and Town Planning Association *(1919)*

¶555

The Wall Street Journal reports that hiking boots are currently the fastest selling item in footwear.

A menswear store in Cambridge, Massachusetts eliminated its entire line of dress shoes to concentrate on hiking boots. Manufacturers of dress and casual shoes are now turning out hiking boots to fill the demand that the traditional hiking boot manufacturers cannot meet.

In addition to the implication of an increased amount of urban walking, the trend suggests greater public acceptance of vehicle-free malls and other limitations on private automobiles.

Wall Street Journal

¶556

A very populous city can rarely, if ever, be well governed.

Aristotle *'Politics'*

¶557

Towns should be built so as to protect their inhabitants and at the same time make them happy.

Aristotle

¶558

If you would be known, and not know, vegetate in a village; if you would know, and not be known, live in a city.

Charles Caleb Colton *'Lacon' (1825)*

¶559

Very excellent things are spoken of thee: thou city of God.

The Book of Common Prayer

¶560

But the present disreputable state of civitas in the United States is the product of an exaggeratedly Calvinist sense of sin. Finding the city irredeemable is only the other side of the coin to expecting it to be Paradise: utopias and dystopias go, of necessity, hand in hand. Disillusion is a vital part of the process of dreaming – and may, one suspects, prove almost as enjoyable.

Jonathan Raban *'Soft City' (1974)*

¶561

As one who long in populous city pent,
Where houses thick and sewers annoy the air,
Forth issuing on a summer's morn to breathe
Among the pleasant villages and farms
Adjoin'd, from each thing met conceives delight.

John Milton *'Paradise Lost'*

¶562

The town is compassed with a high and thick wall, in which there are many towers and forts; there is also a broad and deep dry ditch, set thick with thorns, cast around three sides of the town, and the river is instead of a ditch on the fourth side. The streets are very convenient for all carriage, and are well sheltered from the winds. Their buildings are good, and are so uniform, that a whole side of a street looks like one house. The streets are twenty feet broad; there lie gardens behind all their houses; these are large but enclosed with buildings, that on all hands face the streets; so that every house has both a door to the street and a back door to the garden.

Thomas More *describing the city of Amaurot in 'Utopia' (1515)*

¶563

For the most part the growth of towns was fostered by forces that had no concern for city life as such: the city was the creation of the land speculator, the estate agent, the banker, of the railroad, the tramway and the motor car, of the factory system and of the bureaucratic business organisation.

Lewis Mumford (1963)

¶564

Aristotle's conception that there was a right size for the city, big enough to encompass all its functions, but not too big to interfere with them, was restated in modern times by Howard. He empirically fixed the right number as 30,000 with another 2,000 in the agricultural belt: the same number that Leonardo da Vinci had already hit upon in his proposals for breaking up the clotted disorder of sixteenth century Milan and distributing its citizens into 10 cities of 30,000 each. There is nothing sacred about the number itself.

Lewis Mumford (1963)

¶565

It is in the city, the city as theater, that man's purposive activities are formulated and worked out, through conflicting and cooperating personalities, events, groups, into more significant culminations.

Lewis Mumford *'The Culture of Cities' (1938)*

¶566

As we design our cities for permanent living, not for impermanent financial exploitation, we shall discover, no doubt, a whole series of biological and social constants that will vary little from generation to generation; or at all events, such variation as is necessary will take place within, not in opposition to the permanent form.

Lewis Mumford *'The Culture of Cities' (1938)*

¶567

The city is a fact in nature, like a cave, a run of mackerel or an ant-heap. But it is also a conscious work of art, and it holds within its communal framework many simpler and more personal forms of art. Mind takes form in the city; and in turn, urban forms condition mind. For space, no less than time, is artfully reorganised in cities: in boundary lines and silhouettes, in the fixing of horizontal planes and vertical peaks, in utilizing or denying the natural site, the city records the attitude of a culture and an epoch to the fundamental facts of its existence. The dome and the spire, the open avenue and the closed courts, tell the story, not merely of different physical accommodations, but of essentially different conceptions of man's destiny. The city is both a physical utility for collective living and a symbol of those collective purposes and unanimities that arise under such favouring circumstance. With language itself, it remains man's greatest work of art.

Lewis Mumford *'The Culture of Cities' (1938)*

¶568

American life, in large cities at any rate, is a perpetual assault on the senses and the nerves; it is out of asceticism, out of unworldliness, precisely, that we bear it.

Mary McCarthy

¶569

Every oasis derives its enchantment from the surrounding desert.

Frederick Samson

¶570

They think about Tomorrow, in other words simply about another today; towns have only one day at their disposal which comes back exactly the same every morning.

Jean-Paul Sartre

¶571

Modern architecture has added to our language and had a useful if puritanical purging effect, by its rejection of the status quo and therefore history alienated the movement from cities and urbanism. It is in this area where it has most clearly failed.

Terry Farrell (1984)

¶572

Thanks to British architects, many hundreds of 'Silent Cities of the Dead' have been built in different parts of the world. All are dignified, beautiful and restful and are admired by the foreign peoples in whose land they are. It therefore puzzles me sometimes why so much inferior work has been done in these 20 years for the dwellings of the living in this country which our dead loved and for which they gave their lives.

HRH The Duke of Gloucester *at a Gloucestershire Society Dinner (1938)*

¶573

Cities cannot simply be discarded, like worn-out machinery; they have too large a part in our destiny. But by now it is plain that the life which they have abused is increasingly exacting its revenge, and that this fundamentally, provisional and feverish institution must soon be brought within narrower limits. Whether the work will be done by intelligence or by brute disaster cannot be foreseen.

Sigfried Giedion *'Space, Time and Architecture' (1943)*

¶574

A dome one mile in diameter appropriately skinned may, in future, economically encompass the activity of a city. Such a city would require no weather walls for its individual buildings and yet could be entirely air conditioned.

R Buckminster Fuller *'Ideas and Integrities' (1963)*

¶575

Cities are sensitive, complex organisms which can be seriously harmed by ignorant interference and wholesale renewal. To plan properly for the future we must have a deep understanding of how things came to be as they are and the precise nature of the existing fabric.

Illtyd Harrington *Foreword to 'London Surveyed 1894-1984' (1984)*

¶576

What life have you if you have not life together?
There is no life that is not in community . . .
And now you live dispersed on ribbon roads
And no man knows or cares who is his neighbour
Unless his neighbour makes too much disturbance.
But all dash to and fro in motor cars,
Familiar with the roads and settled nowhere
Nor does the family even move about together.
But every son would have his motorcycle,
And daughters ride away on casual pillions.
When the Stranger says: 'What is the meaning of this City?
Do you huddle close together because you love each other?'
What will you answer? 'We all dwell together
To make money from each other?' or 'This is a community?'

T S Eliot *'The Rock', selected lines*

¶577

Well then; I now do plainly see
This busy world and I shall ne'er agree;
The very honey of all earthly joy
Does of all meats the soonest cloy,
    And they (methinks) deserve my pity,
Who for it can endure the stings,
The crowd, and buz, and murmurings
Of this great hive, the city.

Abraham Cowley *'The Mistress, or Love Verses'*

¶578
I thought it would last my time –
The sense that, beyond the town,
There would always be fields and farms . . .
     Philip Larkin

¶579
The crucial point, however, is that the lesson of modernism can now be treated as
one aesthetic choice among others, and not as a binding historical legacy. The
first casualty of this was the idea that architects or artists can create working
Utopias. Cities are more complex than that, and the needs of those who live in
them less readily quantifiable. What seems obvious now was rank heresy to the
modern movement: the fact that societies cannot be architecturally 'purified'
without a thousand grating invasions of freedom; that the architects' moral
charter, as it were, includes the duty to work with the real world and its inherited
content. Memory is reality. It is better to recycle what exists, to avoid mortgaging
a workable past to a non-existent future, and to think small. In the life of cities,
only conservatism is sanity. It has taken almost a century of modernist claims
and counterclaims to arrive at such a point. But perhaps it was worth the trouble.
     Robert Hughes *'The Shock of the New' (1980)*

¶580
We will neglect our cities at our peril, for in neglecting them we neglect the
nation.
     John F Kennedy *in a message to the US Congress (30 January 1962)*

¶581
Modern architecture is a flop . . . There is no question that our cities are uglier
today than they were fifty years ago.
     Philip Johnson (1968)

¶582
I go among the fields and catch a glimpse of a stoat or a fieldmouse peeping out
of the withered grass – The creature hath a purpose and its eyes are bright with it
– I go amongst the buildings of a city and I see a man hurrying along – to what?
The Creature has a purpose and his eyes are bright with it.
     John Keats *'Letters – to George and Georgina Keats' (19 March 1819)*

¶583
Soft morning, city!
     James Joyce *'Finnegans Wake'*

¶584
Where now the city stands, there was once naught but the city's site.
     Ovid

¶585
The zenith city of the unsalted seas.
Thomas Foster

¶586
I never learned how to tune a harp, or play upon a lute; but I know how to raise a
small and obscure city to glory and greatness Prophetic Mount, whereto all
kindreds of the earth will pilgrim.
Themistocles *on being taunted with his lack of social accomplishments*

¶587
The city is recruited from the country.
George Herbert *'Jacula Prudentum'*

¶588
The village hall was one of those mid-Victorian jobs in glazed red brick which
always seem to bob up in these olde-world hamlets and do so much to encourage
the drift to towns.
P G Wodehouse *'The Mating Season' (1949)*

¶589
Down in the city of sighs and tears, under the white light's glare,
Down in the city of wasted years, you'll find your mamma there.
Andrew B Sterling

¶590
The first requisite to a man's happiness is birth in a famous city.
Euripides *'Plutarch'*

¶591
Servant: Where dwell'st thou?
Coriolanus: Under the canopy . . . I' the city of kites and crows.
William Shakespeare *'Coriolanus'*

¶592
Cities are immortal.
Gratius *'De June Belli et Pacis'*

¶593
The city is of night, but not of sleep;
There sweet sleep is not for the weary brain;
The pitiless hours like years and ages creep,
A night seems termless hell.
James Thomson *'The City of Dreadful Night'*

¶594
In great cities culture is diffused but vulganized.
In great cities proud natures become vain . . . If you want to submerge your own
'I' better the streets of a great city than the solitudes of the wilderness.
Miguel de Unamuno *'Essays and Soliloquies'*

¶595
Come watch with me the azure turn to rose In yonder West:
The changing pageantry,
The fading alps and archipelagoes,
And spectral cities of the sunset-sea.
T B Aldrich *'Miracles'*

¶596
To build up cities an age is needed, but an hour destroys them.
A forest is long in growing, but in a moment is reduced to ashes.
Seneca *'Naturales Questions'*

¶597
Towered cities please us then,
And the busy hum of men.
John Milton *'L'Allegro'*

¶598
Far below and around lay the city like a ragged purple dream, the wonderful,
cruel, enchanting, bewildering, fatal, great city.
O Henry *'Strictly Business'*

¶599
I stood within the City disinterred;
And heard the autumnal leaves like light footfalls
Of spirits passing through the streets; and heard
The Mountain's slumbrous voice at intervals
Thrill through those roofless halls.
Percy Bysshe Shelley *'Ode to Naples'*

¶600
Sun-girt city, thou hast been
Ocean's child, and then his queen;
Now is come a darker day,
And thou soon must be his prey.
Percy Bysshe Shelley *Lines written amongst the Eugenean Hills*

¶601
The City's voice itself is soft like Solitude's.
Percy Bysshe Shelley *Stanzas written in Dejection, near Naples*

¶602
Tell me . . . Have you not observed while walking in this town that among the
buildings which people it, some are dumb, others speak, and yet others, that are
the rarest, sing.
Paul Valéry *'Eupalinos'*

¶603
City wise,
Street wise,
High rise,
Demise.
Don't blame me,
I live out in W3!
    Louis Hellman

¶604
The very turmoil of the streets has something repulsive, something against which human nature rebels. The hundreds of thousands of all classes and ranks crowding past each other, are they not all human beings with the same qualities and powers, and with the same interest in being happy? ... And still they crowd by one another, and their only agreement is the tacit one, that each keep to his own side of the pavement, so as not to delay the opposing streams of the crowd, while it occurs to no man to honor another with so much as a glance.
    Friedrich Engels *'The Condition of the Working Class in England in 1844'*

¶605
Most city diversity is the creation of incredible numbers of different people and different private organisations, with vastly different ideas and purposes, planning and contriving outside the formal framework of public action. The main responsibility of city planning and design should be to develop – insofar as public policy and action can do so – cities that are congenial places for this great range of unofficial plans, ideas and opportunities to flourish, along with the flourishing of the public enterprise.
    Jane Jacobs *'The Death and Life of Great American Cities' (1961)*

¶606
The human animal requires a spatial territory in which to live that possesses unique features, surprises, visual oddities, landmarks and architectural idiosyncrasies. Without them it can have little meaning. A neatly symmetrical, geometric pattern may be useful for holding up a roof, or for facilitating the prefabrication of mass-produced housing units, but when such patterning is applied at the landscape level, it is going against the nature of the human animal. Why else do children prefer to play on rubbish dumps or in derelict buildings, rather than on their immaculate, sterile, geometrically arranged playgrounds?
    Desmond Morris *'The Human Zoo' (1969)*

¶607
Life in the crowded conditions of cities has many attractive features, but in the long run these may be overcome, not so much by altering them, but simply by changing the human race into liking them.
    Charles Darwin

¶608
He gives directions to the town,
To cry it up, or run it down.
Jonathan Swift *'On Poetry'*

¶609
The city is built
To music, therefore never built at all,
And therefore built for ever.
Alfred, Lord Tennyson *'Gareth and Lynette'*

¶610
And ghastly thro' the drizzling rain
On the bald street breaks the blank day.
Alfred, Lord Tennyson *'In Memoriam AHH'*

¶611
Despising,
For you, the city, thus I turn my back:
There is a world elsewhere.
William Shakespeare *'Coriolanus'*

¶612
The City is of Night; perchance of Death,
But certainly of Night.
James Thomson *'The City of Dreadful Night'*

¶613
I dream'd in a dream I saw a city invincible to the attacks of the whole of the rest
of the earth,
I dream'd that was the new city of Friends.
Walt Whitman *'I Dream'd in a Dream'*

¶614
Where women walk in public processions in the streets the same as the men,
Where they enter the public assembly and take places the same as the men;
Where the city of the faithfullest friends stands,
Where the city of the cleanliness of the sexes stands,
Where the city of the healthiest fathers stands,
Where the city of the best-bodied mothers stands,
There the great city stands.
Walt Whitman *'Song of the Broad Axe'*

¶615
Private faces in public places
Are wiser and nicer
Than public faces in private places
W H Auden *'Marginalia'*

¶616
Suburban villas, highway side retreats,
That dread the encroachment of our growing streets,
Tight boxes neatly sash'd, and in a blaze
With all a July sun's collected rays,
Delight the citizen, who, gasping there,
Breathes clouds of dust, and calls it country air.
  William Cowper 'Retirement'

¶617
This world of the suburbs should be entered and explored with due respect and decorum. When the trouble has been taken to uncover some of the romance that lurks behind its shrubberies and to record the sentiments on which the suburban spirit is nourished, then these elusive territories – now the heart of England –past which we unobservantly speed in motor cars and trains and over whose roof-dappled greenery we may all soon be cruising in aeroplanes, will no longer be a strange unknown country.
  Sir James Richards 'The Castles on the Ground' (1946)

¶618
The suburbs are merely vast dormitories, where a man may sleep in comparatively pure air while his office is being washed.
  William McFee 'Casuals of the Sea' (1916)

¶619
Surburbs are things to come into the city from.
  Art Linkletter 'A Child's Garden of Misinformation' (1965)

¶620
Slums may well be breeding grounds of crime, but middle class suburbs are incubators of apathy and delirium.
  Cyril Connolly 'The Unquiet Grave' (1945)

¶621
A ghetto can be improved in one way only: out of existence.
  James Baldwin 'Fifth Avenue, Uptown', in 'Nobody Knows my Name' (1961)

¶622
Slums have their good points; they at least have community spirit and solve the problem of loneliness.
  Sir Basil Spence (1966)

¶623
A mistress should be like a little country retreat near the town, not to dwell in constantly, but only for a night and away.
  William Wycherley 'The Country Wife'

Conservation

¶624
Don't clap too hard – it's a very old building.
John Osborne *'The Entertainer'*

¶625
We should make the old serve the new.
Mao Tse-Tung

¶626
Stop this useless longing for the past. Pass by, we are working for the future since the threads of history are in our hands!
George Bernard Shaw

¶627
Of this I am quite sure, that if we open a quarrel between the past and the present, we shall find we have lost the future.
Sir Winston Churchill (1940)

¶628
Too many people spend too much time looking back with regret and forward with fear that they fail to realise the present is there offering them flowers.
Chinese Proverb *quoted by Michael Manser, in a letter to the 'Sunday Telegraph'* *(27 January 1985)*

¶629

Conservation is a comparatively new idea.

Michael Manser *in 'The Financial Times' (11 January 1984)*

¶630

The bulk of our heritage has got nothing to do with the present conservation movement. It was all there. And what's happening now is conservation has gone to such a length that it's actually inhibiting and holding back the development of a new architecture, a new heritage which the future will enjoy. I think the present trend for preserving elevations only is a terrible thing to do, because if there's nothing in the building that you want to preserve or is fit to preserve except the elevation it becomes a death mask. It's a dreadful thing to do to a town and a stupid thing to do to a building.

Michael Manser

¶631

We must beware of contempt for old buildings just because, like old people, they can be frail, muddled and squalid. That contempt can easily become a sort of architectural fascism. Not all our slums are slums. Piecemeal renewal, each piece in scale with the place, is not necessarily a wrong answer just because it is an old one.

Lionel Brett, Viscount Esher *'Preservation after Buchanan' (1964)*

¶632

If any person for the sake of traffic [i.e. profit] should have purchased any building, in hopes of gaining more by pulling it down than the sum for which he bought it, he shall be obliged to pay into the exchequer double the sum for which he purchased it.

Roman inscription *prior to AD 63 condemning demolition*

¶633

The most cruel kind of traffic in Herculaneum.

Roman inscription *prior to AD 63 condemning demolition*

¶634

The need now is to establish coexistence between past and present creations. As Randolph Langenbach asked in A Future from the Past, 'Is it not better to add to the sum total of the record of human creativity than to subtract from it?' Are there not enough opportunities for new buildings without destroying fine or worthwhile buildings from the past?

Marcus Binney *'Oppression to obsession', in 'Our Past Before Us' (1981)*

¶635

Having to save the old that's worth saving, whether in landscape, houses, manners, institutions or human types, is one of our greatest problems, and the one we bother about least.

John Galsworthy *'Over the River'*

¶636
People gush and moan too much about the loss of ancient buildings of no special note . . . in towns, as in human bodies, the only state of health is one of rapid wasting and repair.

C E Montague *'The Right Place'*

¶637
An architect must perform in the dual role of designer of the future and defender of the past.

Richard England

¶638
Old houses mended,
Cost little less than new, before they're ended.

Colley Cibber *'Double Gallant' Prol l 15*

¶639
All art is a fight against decay.

Brian Aldiss (1971)

¶640
Where can we find greater structural clarity than in the wooden buildings of old? Where else can we find such unity of material, construction and form? Here the wisdom of whole generations is stored. What warmth and beauty they have! They seem to be echoes of old songs.

Ludwig Mies van der Rohe

¶641
There aren't in fact many individual buildings which need to be preserved.

Richard Seifert

¶642
The policy of sweeping clearances should be recognised for what I believe it is: one of the most disastrous and pernicious blunders in the chequered history of sanitation.

Patrick Geddes (*c.* 1915)

¶643
The greatness of an artist is more in the faith of his tradition than in the arrogance of his revolt.

Abdel Wahed El-Wakil

¶644
I honour beginnings, of all things I honour beginnings. I believe that what has always been, and what is has always been, and what will be has always been.

Louis Kahn

¶645

At first, the appearance of antiquity may have served chiefly to make innovation respectable; the English genius for changing content without changing form, for innovating under the cloak of continuity, has often been praised, but as time went on, more and more stress was put on the antiquity of form than on the novelty of content. The carapace, and fascination with it, became an increasingly tighter bond upon the life within.

Martin J. Wiener 'English Culture and the Decline of the Industrial Spirit 1850–1980'

¶646

Some of a city's diversity, historic continuity and character is destroyed when old buildings are razed. The historic significance of architectural styles is as indisputable as the historic events surrounding them. After all, we do not throw out the wedding pictures of our parents because their dress now looks funny, or because the pictures are not quite so wonderful as we once thought they were.

Wolf von Eckardt quoted in 'Time'

¶647

They should turn everywhere into a museum. It is a museum, they just need to put a label on it all.

Yoko Ono quoted in 'Esquire' (1967)

¶648

Engulfed by so much residual evidence of history, a real problem does exist for the British of reconciliation of past with future but the challenge of this conflict gives direction and real architectural opportunity. There are differing views of the past and different weighting given to what remains, but the only genuinely uncreative interpretation is that which argues that the collective memory needs to be erased in order to progress – to recommend denial is, as even Hollywood cowboys remind us, 'running away from oneself'.

Terry Farrell 'British Architecture After Modernism' (1984)

¶649

A commitment to conserving historical memories and patterns adds immeasurably to our lives and the arguments for their demolition on the grounds of 'progress' are quite indefensible; if technology is to add to our lives, then a route via destruction cannot be justified because it impoverishes us.

Terry Farrell 'British Architecture After Modernism' (1984)

¶650

I drove through town to the old house
Where memory is ever new;
But there in the place of the old house
Was the crane and bulldozer crew.
For they're pulling down the old house
To build the motorway
Heading for the year 2,000 and the past
Gets in the way.

Jim Craig 'The Song of the City' – (The Islanders)

651

With the passing of each [historic building] goes a slice of social history – a thread of civilisation. Surely we can learn to reweave those threads in a bright new context, so that our children and grandchildren can respond, as we have, to the challenge of beauty created hundreds of years ago?

The Countess of Dartmouth *'Do You Care about Historic Buildings?' (1970)*

652

The clearest advantage we have today is the experience of yesterday.

R Buckminster Fuller

653

If the design of the building be originally bad, the only virtue it can ever possess will be signs of antiquity.

John Ruskin *'Modern Painters (1843–60)'*

654

It is . . . no question of expediency or feeling whether we shall preserve the buildings of past times or not. We have no right whatever to touch them. They are not ours. They belong partly to those who built them, and partly to all the generations of mankind who are to follow us. The dead have still their right in them.

John Ruskin *'Seven Lamps of Architecture' (1849)*

655

Planning is the means of conservation; it is also the means of total destruction.

Pershore Civic Society, Worcestershire *Evidence given to the UN conference on the Human Environment (June 1972)*

656

He has a passion for Victoriana
Nostalgia flows like lava from his quill
How lovely the remembered dreams of Cornwall!
How long the golden days of Muswell Hill.

Roger Woddis *on Sir John Betjeman, 'Far more than freckled girls', in 'Radio Times' (12 February 1983)*

657

It is a reverend thing to see an ancient castle or building, not in decay.

Francis Bacon *'Essays: Of Nobility'*

¶658

Historic buildings, like businesses, often demand an entrepreneurial approach. Those who see them principally as a burden are of two types. One is the speculator, the developer who wishes to be rid of them for financial gain. The other is the administrator, who grudges the time and money absorbed in looking after older buildings or lacks the expertise, advice or imagination to see how they could be adapted in a practical and economic way. Both types are often obsessed by the idea that a new building replacing the old one will somehow be magically maintenance-free.

Marcus Binney *'Oppression to obsession', in 'Our Past Before Us' (1981)*

¶659

Indolent people with a vested interest in the status quo reject rational enquiry in case they find out too much, since reason leads to understanding, understanding exposes injustice, and injustice calls for dreaded change. Thus reason is rejected not because it failed us – but out of fear that sooner or later it might succeed.

Berthold Lubetkin *RIBA President's invitation lecture (1985)*

¶660

Architectural structures which because of their specific technical features frequently survive for centuries, belong to the basic monuments of the past and the cultural development of the entire nation. At the same time they are evidence of its economic and social development. The works of architecture and town planning thus embody the history of the people that created them. The destruction of these monuments which tells the history of the nation, effaces the traces of the past, weakens a nation, destroys its attachment to tradition and the social roots that have grown for centuries, causes a people to succumb more easily to denationalisation.

Adolf Ciborowski *'Town Planning in Poland 1945–1955'*

¶661

The conservation movement is an expression of the concern that material progress should not be self-defeating.

The Burton St Leonards Society, Sussex *Evidence given to the UN conference on the Human Environment (June 1972)*

¶662

Conservation is bound to involve preservation, but it is more than preservation: it is bringing an area back to life.

Colin Buchanan *'Bath: a Study in Conservation' (1968)*

¶663

To create the future, build on the past.

Richard England

About Building

¶664
How very little, since things were made,
Things have altered in the building trade.
   Rudyard Kipling 'A Truthful Song'

¶665
He builded better than he knew; –
The conscious stone to beauty grew.
   Ralph Waldo Emerson 'The Problem'

¶666
There are many things which we do which don't seem to have any particular
point or tangible result. Take today; a lot of time and energy has been spent on
arranging for you to listen to me take a long time to declare open a building
which everybody knows is open already.
   HRH The Duke of Edinburgh in a speech at the opening of Chesterfield College of
   Technology (21 November 1958)

¶667
   Building is . . .
A thief
A sweet impoverishing
Building and borrowing, a sack full of sorrowing.
Building and marrying of children are great wasters.
The charges of building, and of making gardens, are unknown.
Fools build houses, and wise men buy them.
Who borrows to build, builds to sell.
   Proverbs (the last one Chinese) from 'The Penguin Dictionary of Proverbs'

¶668
Here is a fact that never should be hid:
House painting came before the houses did.
Primitive man, who could not build at all,
Could paint good pictures on his cavern wall.
  A P Herbert

¶669
Yesterday, upon the site,
I saw a wall that wasn't right.
It wasn't right again today;
Tomorrow I shall stay away!
  Peter J Hawker *corruption of 'Last night upon the stair, etc.'*

¶670
A habitation giddy and unsure
Hath he that buildeth on the vulgar heart.
  William Shakespeare *'Henry IV'*

¶671
Confusion now hath made his masterpiece!
Most sacrilegious murder hath broke ope
The lord's annointed temple, and stole thence
The life O' the building!
  William Shakespeare *'Macbeth'*

¶672
The stone which the builders refused is become the head stone of the corner.
  Psalms, cxviii, 22

¶673
. . . and when I say Piles for Piers I don't mean Haemorrhoids for the
H'aristocracy . . .
  Structures lecturer, *Oxford School of Architecture (c. 1969)*

¶674
Bomb squad officers investigating a Birmingham explosion found that an
Irishman had tried to reconnect his gas supply by candlelight.
  Daily Telegraph *(21 November 1975)*

¶675
Old brick layers never die, they just throw in the trowel.
  Anon

Places: Home

¶676
I hate Bath. There is a stupid sameness, notwithstanding the beauties of its buildings.

Benjamin Robert Haydon *'Diary' (August 1809)*

¶677
Bournemouth is one of the few English towns that one can safely call 'her'.

Sir John Betjeman *'First and Last Loves' (1960)*

¶678
The Pavilion at Brighton is like a collection of stone pumpkins and pepper boxes. It seems as if the genius of architecture had at once the dropsy and the *megrims*. Anything more fantastical, with a greater dearth of invention, was never seen. The King's stud (if they were horses of taste) would petition against so irrational a lodging.

William Hazlitt *'Notes of a Journey through France and Italy' (1826)*

¶679
The result of St Paul's having whelped at Brighton.

Sidney Smith *Canon of St Paul's on Brighton Pavilion*

¶680
They dreamt not of a perishable home
Who thus could build.

William Wordsworth *on King's College Chapel, Cambridge (c. 1820)*

¶681

Tax not the Royal Saint with vain expense,
With ill-matched aims the Architect who planned –
Albeit labouring for a scanty band
Of white-robed Scholars only – this immense
And glorious work of fine intelligence!
Give all thou canst; high Heaven rejects the lore
Of nicely-calculated less or more.

    William Wordsworth *on King's College Chapel, Cambridge (c.1820)*

¶682

Mr Simeon . . . took me into King's College Chapel, that celebrated building. He
told me that he had lately compared the size of it with the dimensions of Noah's
Ark as given in the Scripture, and found that the Ark was twice the length, and
twice the breadth, and two-thirds of the height of the Chapel . . . He took me to
the roof of the building and shewed me the admirable manner in which it was
contrived so that stones two yards thick were in the centre tapering off to not
more than two feet. The whole roof is of stone unsupported by beams. – It
remains perfect, there having been no decay. The principle upon which it is
constructed has not been so far discovered as to enable anyone to imitate it. Sir
Christopher Wren said that if He could be shown where the first stone was laid,
he would execute one like it.

    Joseph Farington *on King's College Chapel, Cambridge, in 'Diary' (13 September 1805)*

¶683

Trinity is like a dead body in a high state of putrefaction. The only interest of it
is in the worms that come out of it.

    Lytton Strachey *on Trinity College, Cambridge, in a letter to a friend (1903)*

¶684

It had simply never occurred to me before that day that towns could have a
shape and be, like my beloved locomotives, things with character and meaning.
If you had been drawing 'engines' for years and were then suddenly taken to
such a city, you would instantly see what I mean. I had not been training myself
to see Chichester, the human city, the city of God, the place where life and work
and things were all in one and all in harmony. That, without words, was how it
seemed to me that day. It was not its picturesqueness, for Chichester is the least
picturesque of cathedral cities. It wasn't its antiquity; for I had learned no history
and age meant little to me. It was a town, a city, a thing planned and ordered –
no mere congeries of more or less sordid streets, growing, like a fungus,
wherever the network of railways and sidings and railway sheds would allow.

    Eric Gill *on Chichester, 'Autobiography' (1940)*

¶685
Dear Mary,
Yes, it will be bliss
To go with you by train to Diss,
Your walking shoes upon your feet;
We'll meet, my sweet, at Liverpool Street.
Sir John Betjeman 'A Mind's Journey to Diss'. Addressed to Mrs Harold Wilson
(Lady Wilson)

¶686
During the time I was organist of Exeter Cathedral, a couple of Americans
arrived to visit the cathedral late on a Saturday evening. Told by the verger that
the cathedral was about to close but would open again at seven o'clock in the
morning, the husband turned to his wife and remarked: 'Say, what d'yer know;
this place even opens on a Sunday.'
Dr Lionel Dakers Director of the Royal School of Church Music

¶687
Could not get in at Hastings where the architectural style, according to Leo, is
divided between Early Wedding Cake and Late Water Closet.
James Agate 'Ego 2' (22 August 1936)

¶688
Those twins of learning that he rais'd in you,
Ipswich and Oxford.
William Shakespeare 'Henry VIII'

¶689
Go down to Kew in lilac-time, in lilac-time, in lilac-time;
Go down to Kew in lilac-time (it isn't far from London!)
Alfred Noyes 'Barrel Organ'

¶690
The cathedral is, I believe, the finest building in the whole world.
William Cobbett on Lincoln Cathedral, in 'Rural Rides' (23 April 1830)

¶691
... discussing the merits of the new cathedral, one third built, rising like an
improbable airship out of the sunken graveyard. Last year it had been taller and
the year before taller still.
'They keep knocking it down,' said Meyer, 'and starting all over again. Once it
resembled a child's sandcastle. Whatever it is they're after it seems to evade
them.' Soon, he fancied, the structure might escape altogether; bursting from its
moorings, it would lift, zeppelin-shaped and pink as a rose, into the scudding
clouds.
Beryl Bainbridge on Liverpool Cathedral, 'Young Adolf' (1978)

¶692
They are built as if they were intended to endure as long as the Pyramids.
John Forney *on Liverpool Docks, in 'Letters from Europe' (1867)*

¶693
The streets of London are paved with gold.
Proverb

¶694
You are now
In London, that great sea, whose ebb and flow
At once is deaf and loud, and on the shore
Vomits its wrecks, and still howls on for more.
Yet in its depth what treasures!
Percy Bysshe Shelley *in a letter to Maria Gisborne (July 1820)*

¶695
At length they all to merry London came,
To merry London, my most kindly nurse,
That to me gave this life's first native source.
Edmund Spenser *'Prothalamion' (1596)*

¶696
But now behold,
In the quick forge and working-house of thought,
How London doth pour out her citizens.
William Shakespeare *'Henry V'*

¶697
Ah London! London! our delight,
Great flower that opens but at night,
Great city of the midnight sun,
Whose day begins when day is done.
Richard Le Galliene *'A Ballad of London'*

¶698
Large buildings in London and elsewhere today are too often designed in the lift going down to lunch.
Sir William Holford *quoted in 'Observer,' 'Sayings of the Week' (5 June 1960)*

¶699
Here falling houses thunder on your head,
And here a female atheist talks you dead.
Samuel Johnson *on London*

¶700
When a man is tired of London, he is tired of life; for there is in London all that life can afford.
Samuel Johnson *(20 September 1777)*

¶701

Among the noble cities of the world that Fame celebrates, the City of London of the Kingdom of the English, is the one seat that pours out its fame more widely, sends to farther lands its wealth and trade, lifts its head higher than the rest. It is happy in the healthiness of its air, in the Christian religion, in the strength of its defences, the nature of its site, the honour of its citizens, the modesty of its matrons; pleasant in sports; fruitful of noble men.

William FitzStephen *(c.1180) on London (population then about 40,000). 'Life of Thomas Beckett'*

¶702

I am of the opinion that if, instead of one, we had twelve great cities, so many centres of men, riches and power would be more advantageous than one. For this vast city is like the head of a rickety child.

Fletcher of Saltoun *(1730) on London (population then about 500,000)*

¶703

It is difficult to speak adequately or justly of London. It is not a pleasant place; it is not agreeable or cheerful or easy, or exempt from reproach . . . The fogs, the smoke, the dirt, the darkness, the wet, the distances, the ugliness, the brutal size of the place, the horrible numerosity of society, the manner in which this senseless bigness is fatal to amenity, to convenience, to conversation, to good manners – this and much more you may expatiate upon.

Henry James *(1881) on London (population then 3,814,571) in his 'Journal'*

¶704

London seems to me like some hoary massive underworld, a hoary ponderous inferno. The traffic pours through the rigid grey streets like the rivers of hell . . .

D H Lawrence *'Selected Letters' (1950)*

¶705

I don't know what London's coming to – the higher the building, the lower the morals.

Noël Coward *'Law and Order – Collected Sketches and Lyrics' (1928)*

¶706

London is a nation, not a city.

Benjamin Disraeli

¶707

London is a modern Babylon.

Benjamin Disraeli *'Tancred'*

¶708

London, that great cesspool into which all the loungers of the Empire are irresistibly drained.

Sir Arthur Conan Doyle *'A Study in Scarlet'*

¶709

It is my belief, Watson, founded upon my experience, that the lowest and vilest alleys of London do not present a more dreadful record of sin than does the smiling and beautiful countryside.

Sir Arthur Conan Doyle *'Copper Beeches'*

¶710

It was a Sunday afternoon, wet and cheerless; and a duller spectacle this earth of ours has not to show than a rainy Sunday in London.

Thomas de Quincey *'The Pleasures of Opium'*

¶711

Have you seen anything of London, yet? [Herbert]
  Why, yes: Sir – but we didn't find that it come up to its likeness in the red bills –it is there drawd too architectooralooral. [Joe Gargery]

Charles Dickens *'Great Expectations'*

¶712

London is the epitome of our times, and the Rome of today.

Ralph Waldo Emerson *'English Traits'*

¶713

London is a splendid place to live for those who can get out of it.

Lord Balfour of Burleigh *quoted in 'Observer', 'Sayings of the Week' (1 October 1944)*

¶714

But when his friends did understand
His fond and foolish mind,
They sent him up to fair London,
An apprentice for to bind.

Ballads *'The Bailiff's Daughter of Islington'*

¶715

Hell is a city much like London – a populous and smoky city.

Percy Bysshe Shelley (1819)

¶716

The chief advantage of London is, that a man is always so near his burrow.

Hugo Meynell

¶717

Forget six counties overhung with smoke,
Forget the snorting steam and piston stroke,
Forget the spreading of the hideous town;
Think rather of the pack-horse on the down,
And dream of London, small and white and clean,
The clear Thames bordered by its gardens green.

William Morris *'The Wanderers'*

¶718
Where London's column, pointing at the skies,
Like a tall bully, lifts the head, and lies.
   Alexander Pope *to Lord Bathurst*

¶719
The parks – the lungs of London.
   William Pitt, Earl of Chatham *'The Caretaker'*

¶720
Oh, London is a fine town,
A very famous city,
Where all the streets are paved with gold,
And all the maidens pretty.
   George Colman the Younger *'The Heir at Law'*

¶721
London is chaos incorporated.
   George Mikes *'Down with Everybody'*

¶722
Behold now this vast city; a city of refuge, the mansion-house of liberty,
encompassed and surrounded with His protection.
   John Milton *on London, in 'Areopagitica' (1644)*

¶723
They [railway termini] are out gates to the glorious and the unknown. Through
them we pass out into adventure and sunshine, and to them, alas! we return.
   E M Forster *on London*

¶724
The world believed it impossible to attain magnificence in building without
order, symmetry, and proportion; but the Adams erected the Adelphi and
convinced the world of its mistake.
   Roger Shanhagan *on the Adelphi, London, quoted in 'The Exhibition' (1779)*

¶725
A venerated Queen of Northern Isles reared to the memory of her loving
Consort a monument whereat the nations stand aghast. Is this the reward of
conjugal virtue? Ye husbands, be unfaithful.
   Norman Douglas *on the Albert Memorial, London, quoted in 'An Almanac' (1945)*

¶726
The Albert Hall is a Twelfth Night cake, from which some giant has removed the
ornament off the top and placed it on the other side of the road.
   Anon *on the Royal Albert Hall and Albert Memorial, London*

¶727
Man in the Barbican complex:
Excuse me, could you tell me the best way to get to the theatre?
Cleaning operative:
Well, I wouldn't start from here.
Louis Hellman *on the Barbican, London*

¶728
The tall and portly 'Big Ben' Hall was involved with the building of the Houses of Parliament after a fire in 1834. In September 1856 Parliament was much concerned with the pressing question of a name for the new fourteen-ton bell being installed in the clock tower. 'How about Big Ben?' someone offered. To a man, Parliament rang with delightful applause, and Sir Benjamin's nickname was immortalized.
Sir Benjamin Hall *on the naming of Big Ben, London*

¶729
I must say, notwithstanding the expense which has been incurred in building the palace, no sovereign in Europe, I may even add, perhaps no private gentleman, is so ill lodged as the King of this country.
The Duke of Wellington *on Buckingham Palace, London*

¶730
Uglier structures of the kind there may be many; yet scarcely any one that is more deficient in grandeur and nobleness of aspect.
W H Leeds *on Buckingham Palace, London, in 'Illustrations of the public buildings of London' (1838)*

¶731
Clapham like every other city is built on a volcano.
G K Chesterton *'Autobiography' (1936)*

¶732
The infinite repetition of the same elements – a necessity in such a building – seems to us to debar it from claiming great architectural merit.
Ecclesiologist *on the Crystal Palace, London (1851)*

¶733
This block of glass as monotonous as it is unsightly.
Hector Horeau *on the Crystal Palace, London, quoted in Claude Mignot, 'Architecture of the nineteenth century in Europe'*

¶734
The Crystal Palace – It is like the fragment of a midsummer night's dream seen in the clear light of day.
Lothar Bucher

¶735

Put it under a glass case.

> **Sir Edwin Lutyens** *when asked by a committee what should be done with the Crystal Palace, quoted in 'A Goldfish Bowl' by Elisabeth Lutyens*

¶736

The rows of red brick houses or mansions in Cadogan Square or Lennox Gardens . . . built in a sort of Queen Anne or 17th century Renaissance, show how well we may spoil the best architecture by crowding rows of tall houses together, and how even the most varied elevations may defeat the good intention of the designers. Here we find all kinds of 'cleverness' in picturesque planning, the recessed bay windows, the 'ingle-nook' porch, the wide squat doorway, the small paned window, three panelled door, a variety of quaint bits and details in carved brickwork, all jumbled together in capricious confusion.

> **Building News** *LXII (1892) on the Cadogan and adjacent estates, London*

¶737

Walked and looked at the grand entrance to the Railway. It is extraordinary how decidedly the public have adopted Greek Architecture. Its simplicity, I take it, is suitable to English decision.

> **Benjamin Robert Haydon** *on the Euston Station Arch, London, in his 'Diary'*
> *(27 May 1838)*

¶738

The stone portico of Brobdingnagian proportions [was] not an entrance at all, but a huge mass of useless masonry fit neither for pedestrianism nor vehicle.

> **The Architect** *(1873) on the Euston Arch, London*

¶739

When I made the obvious point about not bombing Rome because the Nazis didn't bomb Athens, whose buildings I said were the equivalent of Shakespeare's plays or Beethoven's symphonies, somebody shouted, 'Wot abaht the 'uman architecture of the Whitechapel Road?'

> **James Agate** *on the East End of London, quoted in 'Ego 6' (14 January 1943)*

¶740

As I walked the streets of this transcendental city, soothed by the sense of order and beautiful architecture all around me, I began to feel that I too was an Idealist, that here was my spiritual home, and that it would be a seemly thing to give up the cinemas and come and make my abode on this hill-top.

> **Logan Pearsall-Smith** *on Hampstead Garden Suburb, London, in 'More Trivia' (1921)*

¶741

I did not fully understand the dread term 'terminal illness' until I saw Heathrow for myself.

> **Dennis Potter** *on Heathrow Airport, London, quoted in 'The Sunday Times'*
> *(4 June 1978)*

¶742

Highbury bore me. Richmond and Kew
Undid me. By Richmond I had raised my knees
Supine on the floor of a narrow canoe.

T S Eliot 'The Fire Sermon'

¶743

One of two or three examples of modern architecture in England . . . that can be
judged by international standards.'

Architectural Review (January 1936) on Highpoint One (1936) by Lubetkin & Tecton

¶744

All the public buildings of the last half century have been behind the average
architectural talent of the day, manifestly because the employment has been
consigned to 'Professional Men'.

Sir Edward Cust MP commenting on the controversial design of the Houses of
Parliament, the subject of an architectural competition in 1835.

¶745

You must build your House of Parliament upon the river; so . . . that the
populace cannot exact their demands by sitting down round you.

The Duke of Wellington, quoted in 'Words on Wellington'

¶746

They are a triumph of modern confectionery.

John Ruskin on the Houses of Parliament, London

¶747

Thy Fields, fair Islington, begin to bear
Unwelcome buildings, and unseemly piles:
The streets are spreading: and The Lord knows where
Improvement's hand will spare Thy neighb'ring stiles:
The rural blandishments of Maiden Lane
And ev'ry day becoming less and less,
While Kilns and Lime roads force us to complain
Of nuisances time only can suppress.
A few more years, and Copenhagen House
Shall cease to charm The tailor and The snob:
And where attornies' clerks in smoke carouse,
Regardless wholly of tomorrow's job.
Some Claremont Row, or Prospect Place shall rise,
Or Terrace, p'rhaps, misnomer'd PARADISE!

J G/William Hone on Islington (25 March 1827)

¶748

It is very distinguished and personal. The tower has a very fine robust diameter. I
don't think anyone could have done it but Sir Basil. But the siting is a disaster.

Sir Frederick Gibberd on Knightsbridge Barracks by Sir Basil Spence

¶749

There's a storm cloud to the westward over Kenton,
There's a line of harbour lights at Perivale,
Is it rounding rough Pentire in a flood of sunset fire
The little fleet of trawlers under sail?

Sir John Betjeman *on Harrow on the Hill*

¶750

... dull, traditional, negative ... cheapness not in itself an architectural virtue ...
worthy, dull and somewhat skimpy ...

Architectural Review *(October 1951) on the Lansbury Estate (1951)*

¶751

Unreal City,
Under the brown fog of a winter dawn,
A crowd flowed over London Bridge, so many,
I had not thought death had undone so many.

T S Eliot *'The Waste Land'*

¶752

The Knight in the triumph of his heart made several reflections on the greatness
of the British Nation; as, that one Englishman could beat three Frenchmen, that
we cou'd never be in danger of Popery so long as we took care of our fleet; that
the Thames was the noblest river in Europe; that London Bridge was a greater
piece of work than any of the Seven Wonders of the World; with many other
honest prejudices which naturally cleave to the heart of a true Englishman.

Joseph Addison

¶753

The man pitched upon [to build the Mansion House] was originally a shipwright
and to do him justice, he appears never to have lost sight of his first profession.
The front of his [i.e. George Dance the elder's] Mansion House has all the
resemblance possible to a deep laden Indiaman, with her stern galleries and
ginger bread work. The stairs and passages are all ladders and gangways and the
superstructure at tops answers pretty accurately to the idea we usually form of
Noah's ark.

James Ralph *in 'A critical review of the public buildings of London and Westminster'*
(1738 2nd ed). (Mansion House was built 1739–42, so he must be commenting on the
drawings of the House)

¶754

Not one of our lately erected buildings has been the object of more general,
unqualified, and invidious censure than this.

W H Leeds *on the National Gallery, London, in 'Illustrations of the public buildings of*
London' (1838)

¶755

A giant glass stump better suited to downtown Chicago than to the City of London.

HRH The Prince of Wales *on the proposed Mansion House Square scheme by Mies van der Rohe (1984)*

¶756

This unhappy structure may be said to have everything it ought not to have, and nothing which it ought to have. It possesses windows without glass, a cupola without size, a portico without height, pepper boxes without pepper, and the finest site in Europe without anything to show upon it.

All the Year Round *on the National Gallery, London*

¶757

A monstrous carbuncle on the face of a much-loved and elegant friend.

HRH The Prince of Wales *on the proposed extension to the National Gallery (1984)*

¶758

[It] is undoubtedly champagne, a slightly sweet champagne, but of good vintage, a trifle heady and contained in a magnum . . . opposition of strong horizontal lines on the body of the theatre . . . equally vigorous verticals marking the foyer . . . . facing is in artificial stone in which the architects have endeavoured to emphasise the cast character of the material. One must admit that it presents a freshness of outlook and a wealth of ideas hitherto strikingly lacking in theatre and cinema exteriors . . .

Architect & Building News *(24 October 1930) on the New Victoria Theatre by W E Trent & E Wamsley Lewis*

¶759

A distorted isochromal triangle, square to nothing of its surroundings . . . an impossible site on which to place any outcome of the human brain except possibly an underground lavatory.

Sir Alfred Gilbert *the designer of Eros, attrib. (1890) on Piccadilly Circus, London*

¶760

[It is] stacked like a pile of green cotton reels.

A J Marshall *on the Post Office Tower*

¶761

Nests of monstrosities.

Augustus W N Pugin *on Nash's façades in Regent Street*

¶762

Vile enough in point of design . . . all have the appearance of having been erected from hasty unrevised sketches. [They displayed] tawdriness and show, and very little richness; a great deal of poverty and meanness, without any approach to simplicity.

Civil Engineer and Architect's Journal *(1838) on Nash's façades in Regent Street*

¶763

The maximum of ornament . . . but the minimum of convenience. They are . . .
violent digressins from true taste . . .

The Builder, *II (1844) on Nash's houses surrounding Regent's Park*

¶764

. . . it suffers from the prime defect of all acutely transitional art: uncertainty of
aesthetic aim. Every isolated criticism of detail, of disposition, of proportion, is
ultimately only one aspect of this basic uncertainty, this wavering sense of
direction . . . The façade towards Portland Place seems to us more severely
afflicted with uncertainty than any other part of the building. The rustications
and crowning cornice strike a classical note, but the distribution of the openings
has not the strict coherence which classicism demands . . .

Architect & Building News *(2 November 1934) on the RIBA building (1932–34) by*
Grey Wornum

¶765

This is Soho, where anything goes, and just make sure it is not your wallet.

Len Deighton

¶766

The chief architectural inspiration for the pile of concrete blocks on the South
Bank appears to have been a cross between Speer's Atlantic Wall and the
Führerbunker.

Christopher Booker *'Dreams that crack like concrete' (1976)*

¶767

A particularly exciting project would be to convert the South Bank culture estate
by adding, say, 1,000 dwellings, a shopping complex and pubs onto the same
land presently occupied by the National Theatre, Hayward buildings and Festival
Hall. The terraces and riverside could be exploited as amenities and leisure
resources would then be valued to a fuller extent 24 hours a day!

Terry Farrell *'Buildings as a Resource', in 'RIBA Journal' (May 1976)*

¶768

Stafford House, the London house of the Duke and Duchess of Sutherland, was
the centre of high society in the early years of Queen Victoria's reign. The
duchess was a close friend of the Queen. The magnificence of Stafford House
led Victoria to remark to her hostess on one of her frequent visits, 'I have come
from my house to your palace.'

HRH Queen Victoria

¶769

Encroaching as it did most inconveniently, upon one of the most frequented thoroughfares in the metropolis, the former church [of St Dunstan in the West] pointed itself out very markedly to be an obstruction whose removal would be a public advantage; and, fortunately, there was nothing whatever in the structure itself that could cause anyone, hardly the most inveterate antiquarian of the Pennant tribe, to regret its loss, it being, in point of architecture, a medley of unredeemed ugliness.

W H Leeds *'Illustrations of the public buildings of London' (1838)*

¶770

Si Monumentum Requiris, Circumspice

If you seek my monument, look around you

Sir Christopher Wren's son *in the inscription on the architect's memorial in St Paul's Cathedral*

¶771

There is no relief or quiet in any part of the work. The eye is constantly troubled and tormented, and the mechanical patterns follow one another with such rapidity and perseverance, that the mind becomes irritated where it ought to be gratified and goaded to criticism where it should be led calmly to approve. There is here a complete travesty of noble associations, and not the slightest care to save those from sordid contact. An elaboration that might be suitable for a chapter-house, or a Cathedral choir is used as an 'advertising medium' for bagmen's bedrooms and the costly discomforts of a terminus hotel, and the architect is thus a mere expensive rival of the Company's head cook in catering for the low enjoyments of the great travelling crowd . . .

J M Emmett *on St Pancras Station, quoted in 'Victorian Architecture' by Sir John Summerson*

¶772

Here the public taste has been exactly suited, and every kind of architectural decoration has been made thoroughly common and unclean.

J M Emmett *on St Pancras Station, quoted in 'Victorian Architecture' by Sir John Summerson*

¶773

St Pancras was a fourteen-year-old Christian boy, who was martyred in Rome in AD 304 by the Emperor Diocletian. In England he is better known as a railway station.

Sir John Betjeman (1972)

¶774

Karl Marx wasn't a Marxist all the time. He got drunk in the Tottenham Court Road.

Michael Foot *quoted by Susan Barnes in 'Behind the Image'*

¶775

... its projectors have chosen to clothe it with an architectural garb and to make an appeal for admiration for it as an architectural structure; and in this sense it is one of the worst and most ludicrous failures we know of ... The sides of the towers are pierced with a number of windows that light nothing, with gewgaw 'Gothic' decorations ... the towers are about as choice specimens of architectural gimcrack on a large scale as one could wish to see ... The stone gateway of approach ... is ... rendered absurd by the sight of the immense chains which are made to seem as if hanging over it and rove through openings in the masonry, though we know perfectly well that the masonry which is made to appear to carry them would be dragged to pieces even by such movements of the chain as might be caused by expansion and contraction of the metal. By a similar absurdity, the upper ends of the chains are made to appear as if these masonry towers are actually built on and carried by the iron work ... the whole structure is the most monstrous and preposterous architectural sham that we have ever known of, and it is in that sense a discredit to the generation which has erected it ... an elaborate and costly make-believe.

The Builder *(30 June 1894) on Tower Bridge (1886-1894) by Sir Horace Jones*

¶776

The whole thing as far as architectural expression is concerned is the most colossal architectural gimcrack that has ever been seen.

H H Statham *on Tower Bridge, in 'The Builder' (23 February 1895)*

¶777

If Nelson looks down on a couple of Kings,
However it pleases the Loyals;
Tis after the fashion of nautical things
A Sky-scraper over the Royals.

Thomas Hood *Epigram on the 'Arrangement of the Statues in Trafalgar Square' (1844)*

¶778

Behold, ye builders, demigods who made England's Walhalla.

Theodore Watts-Dunton *on Westminster Abbey in 'The Minster Spirits'*

¶779

That the Cause of the Departing Pier's sinking is nothing else but the effect of unparalleled Gross Ignorance, Madness, or Knavery: for none but a Fool, a Madman, or a Knave would have built it, on a foundation which was known ... to be infirm.

Batty Langley *'A survey of Westminster Bridge' (1748)*

¶780

Earth has not anything to show more fair;
Dull would be the soul who could pass by
A sight so touching in its majesty:
This City now doth, like a garment, wear
The beauty of the morning; silent, bare,
Ships, towers, domes, theatres, and temples lie
Open unto the fields, and to the sky;
All bright and glittering in the smokeless air.

William Wordsworth *'Upon Westminster Bridge' (1802)*

¶781

A gasometer and a water tower.

Anon *on the Roman Catholic Cathedral of Westminster by Bentley*

¶782

An acre in Middlesex is better than a principality in Utopia.

Lord Macaulay *to Lord Bacon*

¶783

I had always assumed that cliché was a suburb of Paris, until I discovered it to be
a street in Oxford.

Philip Guedalla

¶784

And that sweet City with her dreaming spires,
She needs not June for beauty's heightening.

Matthew Arnold *on Oxford, 'Thyrsis'*

¶785

Cambridge sees Oxford as the Latin quarter of Cowley.

Marjorie Knight *in a letter to 'The Daily Telegraph' (15 August 1979)*

¶786

Noon strikes in England, Noon on Oxford town
Beauty she was statue cold – there's blood upon her gown
Noon of my dreams, O noon!
Proud and godly kings had built her long ago
With her towers and tombs and statues all around
With her fair and floral air, and the love that lingers there
And the streets where the dead men go.

James Elroy Flecker *'The Dying Patriot'*

¶787

Come, friendly bombs, and fall on Slough!

Sir John Betjeman *first line of 'Slough'*

¶788

Sheffield, I suppose, could justly claim to be called the ugliest town in the Old World: its inhabitants, who want it to be pre-eminent in everything, very likely do make that claim for it.

George Orwell

¶789

You come over here [i.e. to Britain] and you find the best modern architecture in the world.

Philip Johnson

¶790

And did those feet in ancient time
Walk upon England's Mountains green?
And was the holy lamb of God
On Englands pleasant pastures seen?
And did the Countenance divine
Shine forth upon our clouded Hills?
And was Jerusalem builded here
Among those dark satanic Mills?

William Blake *'Milton' preface*

¶791

It will be said of this generation that it found England a land of beauty and left it a land of beauty spots.

C E M Joad *quoted in 'Observer', 'Sayings of the Week' (31 May 1953)*

¶792

Earth proudly wears the Parthenon,
As the best gem upon her zone,
And Morning opes with haste her lids
To gaze upon the Pyramids;
O'er England's abbeys bends the sky,
As on its friends, with kindred eye;
For out of Thought's interior sphere
These wonders rose to upper air;
And Nature gladly gave them place,
Adopted them into her race,
And granted them with an equal date
With Andes and with Ararat.

Ralph Waldo Emerson *'The Problem'*

¶793

There was King Bradmond's palace,
Was never none richer, the story says:
For all the windows and the walls
Were painted with gold, both towers and halls;
Pillars and doors all were of brass;
Windows of latten were set with glass;
It was so rich, in many wise,
That it was like a paradise.

Anon *'Sir Bevis of Hampton' (c. 1325)*

¶794

Most of the geography of Scotland consists of mountains, grass, heather and
Edinburgh.

Frank Muir

Places: Abroad

¶795

In settling an island, the first building erected by a Spaniard will be a church; by a Frenchman a fort; by a Dutchman a warehouse; and by an Englishman an alehouse.

Proverb

¶796

Travelling architectural consultants are cultural or technocratic mercenaries, hired intellectual 'guns' who move around the world giving counsel . . . mercenaries without uniforms . . . but potentially just as lethal.

Jacquelin T Robertson

¶797

Architecture does not travel well.

Richard England

¶798

Thousands of slaves died building the ziggurats
They didn't have unions, paid overtime or hard hats,
That's why you see carved on the sides of this wealth,
ZIGGURATS CAN SERIOUSLY DAMAGE YOUR HEALTH.

Louis Hellman

¶799

That far land we dream about, where every man is his own architect.

Robert Browning *'Red Cotton Nightcap Country'*

¶800

We are going to call our legacy from the Past, this greater free city for the Individual, Broadacre City, simply because it is broadly based upon the spacing of the minimum of an acre, or several, to an individual. But more important, because when Democracy builds – this is the City of Democracy . . . In this Free City coming of age of the individual house of the individual family-group will be far more directly related to landscape, transport, distribution of goods, publicity and all cultural opportunity than at present. But it is the Home that will enjoy a freedom and freshness of life from within that no civilisation ever has attained or could ever attain until now.

Frank Lloyd Wright *'When Democracy Builds' (1945)*

¶801

The greatest public-relations building since the pyramids.

Billy Wentworth Sydney MP *on Sydney Opera House, in 'Land of Fortune' by Jonathan Aitken (1971)*

¶802

The sight of it from a high floor of the Hotel Nacional is like a strident chord in a desert of silence. Everything about it is *insolite*: a building here, a building there, receding in a clear, hand-painted Daliesque perspective to an improbable horizon, very minute and distant. Red, red earth. Spectacular underpasses and flyovers and endless avenues of brilliant, contemporary lamp-posts which, at night, create an illusion of a vast inhabited metropolis, instead of the inspired, under-populated lunacy one sees by day. Here and there, workmen are busy, encouraging the visitor to hope that one day, perhaps, Brasilia will be completed.

Brian Crozier *on Brasilia, Brazil, 'Latin American Journey', in 'Encounter' (December 1964)*

¶803

We drove through the impersonal and sinister streets of Brasilia, that terrifying preview of a collectivist future.

Arthur M Schlesinger *'One Thousand Days' (1965)*

¶804

Though the latitude's rather uncertain,
And the longitude also is vague,
The persons I pity who know not the city,
The beautiful city of Prague.

William Jeffrey Prowse *on Prague, in 'My Europe' (1952)*

¶805

It was, I knew afresh, the most beautiful city after Edinburgh that I should ever see.

R H Bruce Lockhart *on Prague, in 'My Europe' (1952)*

¶806

The mighty pyramids of stone
That wedge-like cleave the desert airs,
When nearer seen and better known,
Are but gigantic flights of stairs.

H W Longfellow *on the Pyramids, in 'The Ladder of St Augustine' (1850)*

¶807

Napoleon first demanded to know the measurement of the Great Pyramid: and then astonished his staff on their return from climbing to the top by pointing out that its cubic content would suffice to build a wall ten feet high and a foot thick entirely surrounding France. This is one way of bringing home its staggering bulk.

Julian Huxley *on the Pyramids, in 'From an Antique Land' (1954)*

¶808

They form the Hyde Park Corner of the Middle East.

Lawrence Durrell *on the Pyramids, quoted in 'Radio Times' (8-14 April 1978)*

¶809

The Great Pyramid invites one to do nothing except acknowledge it . . . Its sole interest lies in its size. It is a simple-minded megalomaniac's dream come true. All the subtelty of engineering which went into its construction − the levelling of the ground, the dizzying calculus of stress and weight and proportion – was dedicated to the service of a fantasy so crude that a human vegetable could have conceived it. It exists below the level of reason. Its contempt for money, labour, time, materials, its blind disregard of limitation or compromise, could be matched by any psychopath in a locked ward for the severely subnormal. All the Great Pyramid does is stand between you and the sun, like a mindless giant with his thumbs locked in his hip-pockets, saying, 'OK?'

Jonathan Raban *'Arabia through the Looking Glass' (1979)*

¶810

It was a beautiful evening, and the ruins of the ancient temple, redolent with age, looked most impressive lit up by the setting sun. The tourists gazed at them in awe. 'How old are the ruins?' one of them ventured to ask the local guide. '4,007 years,' came the prompt reply. 'But how can you be sure of the precise year?' asked the tourist.

'Oh', said the guide, 'the leader of the team who excavated the ruins told us that they were 4,000 years old – and that was seven years ago.'

Lord Allen of Abbeydale

¶811

When I lately stood with a friend before [the cathedral of] Amiens, . . . he asked me how it happens that we can no longer build such piles? I replied: 'Dear Alphonse, men in those days had convictions (Ueberzeugungen), we moderns have opinions (Meinungen) and it requires something more than an opinion to build a Gothic cathedral.'

Heinrich Heine *in confidential letters to August Lewald*

¶812

Pessac was conceived to be built of reinforced concrete. The aim: low cost. The means: reinforced concrete. The method: standardization, industrialization, tailorised mass production.

Le Corbusier *on his housing at Cité Fruges, Pessac, near Bordeaux, completed in 1926*

¶813

I think Marseilles may be one of the greatest buildings of all times . . . if you don't go there too often. Under the pilotis is one hell of a place to be unless you want to pee.

Philip Johnson *on Le Corbusier's Unité d'habitation*

¶814

Mankind was never so happily inspired as when it made a cathedral: a thing as single and specious as a statue to the first glance, and yet on examination, as lively and interesting as a forest in detail.

R L Stevenson *on Noyon Cathedral, in 'An Inland Voyage'*

¶815

To err is human, To loaf is Parisian.

Victor Hugo *'Les Misérables' (1862)*

¶816

What would the new boulevards of white stone be without the softening and refreshing aid of those long lanes of well cared-for trees that everywhere rise around the buildings, helping them somewhat as the grass does the buttercups . . In Paris, public gardening assumes an importance which it does not possess with us . . . It follows the street builders with trees, turns the little squares into gardens unsurpassed for good taste and beauty . . .

W Robinson *'The Parks, Promenades, and Gardens of Paris' (1869)*

¶817

Parasite: A person who lives in Paris.

Anon

¶818

It is the ugliest beastly town in the universe.

Horace Walpole *on Paris, in a letter to Thomas Gray (19 November 1765)*

¶819

A loud modern New York of a place.

Ralph Waldo Emerson *on Paris, in his 'Journal' (July 1833)*

¶820

Of all great cities, Paris is the most tolerable in hot weather. It is true that the asphalt liquefies, and it is true that the brilliant limestone of which the city is built reflects the sun with uncomfortable fierceness. It is also true that of a summer evening you pay a penalty for living in the best-lighted capital in the world. The inordinate amount of gas in the streets makes the atmosphere hot and thick, so that even under the dim constellations you feel on a July night as if you were in a high music-hall. If you look down at such a time upon the central portions of Paris from a high window in a remoter quarter, you see them wrapped in a lurid haze, of the devil's own brewing.

Henry James *on Paris, in 'Portraits of Places' (1883) (written in Rouen 1876)*

¶821

Paris is still monumental and handsome. Along the rivers where its splendours are, there's no denying its man-made beauty. The poor, pale little Seine runs rapidly north to the sea, the sky is pale, pale jade overhead, greenish and Parisian, the trees of black wire stand in rows, and flourish their backwire brushes against a low sky of jade-pale cobwebs, and the huge dark-grey palaces rear up their masses of stone and slope off towards the sky still with a massive, satisfying suggestion of pyramids. There is something noble and man-made about it all.

D H Lawrence *'Paris Letter – Laughing Horse' (April 1926)*

¶822

Paris is bogus in its lack of genuine nationality. No one can feel a foreigner on Monte Carlo, but Paris is cosmopolitan in the diametrically opposite sense, that it makes everyone a foreigner. London, deficient as it is in all the attributes which make a town habitable, is at least British. It is our own family skeleton in our own cupboard. Bath and Wells and Birmingham are all implied in London in a way in which Tours or Tarascon or Lyons are not implicit in Paris; the febrile ardours of French provincial life, the tenacity and avarice and logic and militancy of the French character, seem out of place and improbable in the French capital. And sensitive Frenchmen confess to a feeling of awkwardness there . . . It is in Paris that money must be made, but it is best spent in the provinces.

Evelyn Waugh *'Labels' (1930)*

¶823

Paris is like myself a haughty ruin or if you like a decayed reveller.

James Joyce *in a letter to Harriet Shaw Weaver, Paris (1 May 1935)*

¶824

I've been to Paris France and I've been to Paris Paramount. Paris Paramount is better.

Ernst Lubitsch *quoted by Leslie Halliwell, in 'The Filmgoer's Book of Quotes' (1979)*

¶825

If you are lucky enough to have lived in Paris as a young man, then wherever you go for the rest of your life, it stays with you, for Paris is a moveable feast.

Ernest Hemingway *in a letter to a friend (1950)*

¶826

I saw through my window the Eiffel Tower like a flask of clear water, the domes of the Invalides and the Pantheon as a teapot and sugar basin, and the Sacré Cœur a pink and white sugarplum. Delauney came almost every day to visit me. He was always haunted by the tower.

Blaise Cendrars *on the Parisian painter Robert Delauney referring to the Eiffel Tower, in 'Aujourd'hui'*

¶827

During William Morris's last visit to Paris, he spent much of his time in the restaurant of the Eiffel Tower, either eating or writing. When a friend observed that he must be very impressed by the tower to spend so much time there, Morris snorted, 'Impressed! I remain here because it's the only place in Paris where I can avoid seeing the damn thing.'

William Morris

¶828

I ought to be jealous of that tower. She is more famous than I am.

Gustave Eiffel *on the Eiffel Tower*

¶829

It seems to be saying perpetually; 'I am the end of the nineteenth century; I am glad they built me of iron; let me rust.' . . . It is like a passing fool in a crowd of the University, a buffoon in the hall; for of all the things that Paris has made, it alone has neither wits nor soul.

Hilaire Belloc *on the Eiffel Tower (1900)*

¶830

Bernini's design of the Louvre I would have given my Skin for, but the old reserv'd Italian gave me a few Minutes View.

Sir Christopher Wren *in a letter to a friend (1665)*

¶831

What need hast thou of a monument? Thou hast raised to thyself the most glorious one! And though the ants that scrabble around it trouble not about thy name, thou hast a fate like to the master-builder's who piled the mountainpeaks up into the clouds! To few was it granted to conceive in their souls Babel-like thoughts, complete gigantic, wholly lovely down to the finest part, like the trees of God; to fewer still, to light upon thousands of willing hands, to dig out stony foundations, to conjure towering structures thereupon, and then in dying to say to their sons: I am with you always in the works of my spirit — carry out that which I have begun to its consummation, high in the clouds!

J W von Goethe *on Strasbourg Cathedral, in 'Von Deutscher Baukunst' (1772)*

9832

That hallow'd spire which rises to the skies,
Fills ev'ry heart with rapture and surprise;
Approach the temple – round its rev'rend base
Vile traffic shops God's edifice disgrace.
Are there still Goths in this enlightened age
Who dare oppose and scorn the sacred page?
Who by one impious act at once express
Their want of virtue, taste and righteousness?

    David Garrick *upon seeing Strasbourg Cathedral, in 'Extempore by a Stranger' (1764)*

9833

No bombardment can do anything like the damage that the last restoration did.

    Roger Fry *on Rheims Cathedral*

9834

The palace is a huge heap of littleness . . . It ought to be one of the most striking effects of human power and art. I doubt whether there be anywhere any single architectural composition of equal extent . . . yet there are a dozen country houses of private individuals in England alone which have a greater air of majesty and splendour than this huge quarry.

    T B Macaulay *on Versailles, in 'Journal' (2 February 1939) from 'Life and Letters' by G O Trevelyan (1876)*

9835

Versailles was, in practical function, a vast dormitory for the French nobility.

    John Kenneth Galbraith *'Economics, Peace, and Laughter' (1971)*

9836

The Women, as they make here the Language and fashions and meddle in Politicks and Philosophy, so they sway also in Architecture . . . but Building certainly ought to have the Attribute of eternal, and therefore the only Thing uncapable of new Fashions.

    Sir Christopher Wren *in a letter to a friend after seeing the building of Versailles (1665)*

9837

The Wall is a kind of masterpiece of the squalid, the cruel and the hideous, the most naked assertion one could find anywhere that life was not intended to be anything but nasty, brutish, and short. It is quite incredibly ugly, being built of a kind of porous concrete brick that is altogether greyer darker dreader, less responsive to light and shade than any material has any right to be.

    Goronwy Rees *on the Berlin Wall, 'Diary from Berlin to Munich', in 'Encounter' (April 1964)*

9838

I have seen the famous Cathedral, which is a fine building, but not half finished, and as such, an uncomfortable sight, for it looks like a broken promise to God.

    Thomas Hood *on Cologne Cathedral, in 'Up the Rhine' (1840)*

¶839

We spent an hour in the cathedral, which I will not attempt to describe further than by saying it was the most beautiful of all the churches I have ever seen, or can imagine. If one could imagine the spirit of devotion embodied in any material form, it would be in such a building.

Lewis Carroll *on Cologne Cathedral, in 'Diary' (July 1867)*

¶840

In Kohln, a town of monks and bones,
And pavements fang'd with murderous stones
And rags, and hags, and hideous wenches;
I counted two and seventy stenches,
All well defined, and several stinks!
Ye Nymphs that reign o'er sewers and sinks,
The river Rhine, it is well known,
Doth wash your city of Cologne;
But tell me, Nymphs, what power divine
Shall henceforth wash the river Rhine?

Samuel Taylor Coleridge *'Cologne'*

¶841

When God made Frankfurt-am-Main, he shat a lump of concrete.

Günter Grass *quoted by Nigel Dennis in 'New York Review of Books' (23 November 1978) reviewing Grass's 'The Flounder'*

¶842

Art Nouveau ... was born in Munich. Its parent on the male side was Japanese, on the female side a bastard descendant of William Morris via Maple. It was brought up in Germany, fostered by what are called decadent artists. These are artists whose works are a mixture of beer and sausage and Aubrey Beardsley.

Maurice Baring *on Munich, in 'Round the World in Any Number of Days' (1913)*

¶843

The dirtiest and most detestable spot in existence.

Lord Byron *on Gibraltar, in a letter to John Hanson (7 August 1809)*

¶844

It ... is suggestive of a 'gob' of mud on the end of a shingle.

Mark Twain *on Gibraltar, in 'The Innocents Abroad' (1869)*

¶845

The woman motorist touring Europe posed for a souvenir snapshot before the fallen pillars of an historic ruin in Greece. 'Don't get the car in the picture,' she said, 'or my husband will swear I ran into the place!'

Anon

¶846

Acropolis – blocks of marble like sticks of Wenham ice – or like huge cakes of wax.

Parthenon – elevated like cross of Constantine. Strange contrast of rugged rock with polished temple. At Stirling – art & nature correspond. Not so at Acropolis.

Herman Melville *on the Acropolis, Athens, in 'Journal of a Visit to Europe and the Levant' (8 February 1857)*

¶847

It's a lovely spot. We have got all Athens in our arc of fire.

Paratroop Officer's *remark to Lord Moran (December 1944), in 'The Struggle for Survival' by Winston Churchill (1966)*

¶848

A thing of beauty that is a joy once or twice, and afterwards a standing reproach.

Cyril Connolly *on the Acropolis, in 'The Condemned Playground' (1945)*

¶849

Above the low roofs of Athens the Acropolis rises on its pedestal of rock: astonishing, dramatic, divine, with at the same time the look of a phantom.

Edmund Wilson *'Europe without Baedeker' (1947)*

¶850

As the Englishman leaned out of the carriage he saw first an opal-tinted cloud on the horizon, and, later, certain towers. The mists lay on the ground, so that the splendour seemed to be floating free of the earth; and the mists rose in the background, so that at no time could everything be seen clearly. Then as the train sped forward, and the mists shifted, and the sun shone upon the mists, the Taj took a hundred new shapes, each perfect and each beyond description. It was the Ivory Gate through which all good dreams come; it was the realisation of the gleaming halls of dawn that Tennyson sighs of; it was veritably the 'aspiration fixed', the 'sigh made stone' of a lesser poet; and over and above concrete comparisons, it seemed the embodiment of all things pure, all things holy, and all things unhappy. That was the mystery of the building.

Rudyard Kipling *on the Taj Mahal, in 'From Sea to Sea' (1897)*

¶851

Robin Day . . . and I travelled together to see the Taj Mahal a couple of years ago, which gave rise to a notable exchange . . . I said that since his wife was not with him I claimed the right to be her surrogate and ask him a question she would have been entitled to put if she had been present in person. He gravely accepted my claim, and bade me ask. 'Darling,' I said, waving a hand at Shah Jehan's creation, 'do you love me so much that if I were to die you would build something like this in my memory?' Robin considered the question carefully. Then, 'Only if I could get it off tax,' he replied.

Bernard Levin *on the Taj Mahal, in 'The Difference a Day Makes', 'The Times' (16 October 1980)*

¶852

After many exasperating quarrels with Herbert Baker, Lutyens described the Delhi buildings as his Bakerloo.

Sir Edwin Lutyens

¶853

The Viceroy thinks only of what the place will look like in three years time, three hundred is what I think of.

Sir Nikolaus Pevsner *'Lutyens on Delhi'*

¶854

What did these vain and presumptuous men intend? How did they expect to raise this lofty mass against God, when they had built it above all the mountains and clouds of the earth's atmosphere?

Saint Augustine *on Babylon, Iraq, in 'City of God' Book XV*

¶855

Limerick was, Dublin is, and Cork shall be, the finest of the three.

Proverb

¶856

No man saw the building of the New Jerusalem, the workmen crowded together, the unfinished walls and unpaved streets; no man heard the clink of trowel and pickaxe; it descended out of heaven from God.

John Robert Seeley *'Ecce Homo', Ch xxiv*

¶857

No hammers fell, no ponderous axes rung,
Like some tall palm the mystic fabric sprung.

Reginald Heber *'Palestine' l 163 Bishop Heber is describing the building of Solomon's temple*

¶858

On a visit to Israel as mayor of West Berlin, Brandt was invited to view the great new Mann auditorium in Tel Aviv. Having expressed his appreciation of Israel's naming the concert hall for Thomas Mann, the German writer, Brandt was politely corrected by his host. The hall was actually named for a certain Frederic Mann of Philadelphia. 'What did he ever write?' exclaimed Brandt. 'A cheque,' came the reply.

Willy Brandt

¶859

Travelling is the ruin of all happiness!
There's no looking at a building here after seeing Italy.

Fanny Burney (Mme D'Arblay) *'Cecilia' IV Ch 2*

¶860

Henry Moore has just built himself a house there. I could imagine the house — a massive structure in the Lloyd Wright tradition, thrusting out from the side of some huge outcrop with a vista of sky and sea and plain . . . It is (in fact) a red-tiled green shuttered bungalow, with a studio attached in the suburbs of Forte dei Marmi — a kind of Italian Eastbourne.

Nigel Gosling *on Italy, in 'Observer Colour Supplement' (11 September 1966)*

¶861

Giotto's tower, The lily of Florence blossoming in stone.

H W Longfellow *on Giotto's Tower*

¶862

Magnificently stern and sombre are the streets of beautiful Florence; and the strong old piles of building make such heaps of shadow, on the ground and in the river, that there is another and different city of rich forms and fancies, always lying at our feet.

Charles Dickens *on Florence, in 'Pictures from Italy' (1846)*

¶863

In my way home, I looked into the cathedral, an enormous fabric, inlaid with the richest marbles, and covered with stars and chequered work, like an old-fashioned cabinet. The architect seems to have turned his building inside out; nothing in art being more ornamented than the exterior, and few churches so simple within.

William Beckford *on The Duomo, Florence, in 'Dreams Waking Thoughts and Incidents' (1783)*

¶864

Florence is the most enchanting place I know in the world . . . The Cathedral outside (not inside) is to my feeling the most beautiful church in the world, and it always looked to me like a hen gathering its chickens under its wings, it stands in such a soft, lovely way, with Florence round it.

Matthew Arnold *on The Duomo, Florence in a letter to his sister (13 October 1879)*

¶865

Taddeo Gaddi built me. I am old;
Five centuries old. I plant my foot of stone
Upon the Arno, as St Michael's own
Was planted on the Dragon. Fold by fold
Beneath me as it struggles, I behold
Its glistening scales. Twice hath it overthrown
My kindred and companions. Me alone
It moveth not, but is by me controlled.
I can remember when the Medici
Were driven from Florence; longer still ago
The final wars of Ghibelline and Guelf.
Florence adorns me with her jewelry;

And when I think that Michael Angelo
Hath leaned on me, I glory in myself.
>   **H W Longfellow** *on The Ponte-Vecchio, Florence, in 'The Old Bridge at Florence' (1874)*

¶866
The Campanile . . . stands alone on the right side of the Domo or Cathedrall,
strangely remarkable for this, that the beholder would expect every moment
when it should fall; being built exceedingly declining by a rare adresse of the
imortal Architect: and really I take it to be one of the most singular pieces of
workmanship in the World; how it is supported from immediately falling would
puzzle a good Geometrician.
>   **John Evelyn** *on the Leaning Tower of Pisa, in 'Diary' (20 October 1644)*

¶867
I found Rome brick and I left it marble.
[This saying is given another meaning when applied to Caesar's consolidation of
the Government in the following form: 'That Rome, which I found built of mud, I
shall leave you firm as rock.']
>   **Augustus Caesar**

¶868
The hand that rounded Peter's dome,
And groined the aisles of Christian Rome,
Wrought in a sad sincerity;
Himself from God he could not free:
He builded better than he knew; —
The conscious stone to beauty grew.
>   **Ralph Waldo Emerson** *'The Problem'*

¶869
A city for sale, and doomed to speedy destruction, if it finds a purchaser.
>   **Jugurtha** *looking back at Rome, as he left it.*

¶870
Pretending to be disgusted by the drab old buildings and narrow, winding streets
of Rome, he brazenly set fire to the City; and though a group of ex-consuls
caught his attendants, armed with oakum and blazing torches, trespassing on
their property, they dared not interfere. He also coveted the sites of several
granaries, solidly built in stone, near the Golden House [Nero's Palace]; having
knocked down their walls with siege-engines, he set the interiors ablaze. This
terror lasted for six days and seven nights, causing many people to take shelter in
the tombs . . . Nero watched the conflagration from the Tower of Maecenas,
enraptured by what he called 'the beauty of the flames'; then put on his
tragedian's costume and sang The Fall of Ilium from beginning to end."
[Hence the phrase 'fiddling while Rome burns'. Modern historians exonerate

Nero for starting this catastrophic blaze; he himself thought the Christians were the most likely incendiaries — after all, they believed that the end of the world would come with fire — and he persecuted them with much cruelty.]

Gaius Suetonius *tells the story of the burning of Rome by Nero*

¶871

The ruins of Rome existed but they had been hardly seen for a thousand years.

W R Lethaby

¶872

There was once upon a time an Englishwoman who came out to Rome to live there. She was the wife of a scholar who had rooms in the Vatican itself, and she herself lived in a neighbouring Palazzo. She was asked by one of her compatriots whether she liked Rome. She said it was a great come-down after what she had been used to.
'And where', asked the second Englishwoman, 'used you to live in England?'
'Surbiton,' she answered.

Maurice Baring *on Rome, in 'Around the World in Any Number of Days' (1913)*

¶873

While stands the Coliseum, Rome shall stand;
When falls the Coliseum, Rome shall fall;
And when Rome falls — the World.

Lord Byron *on the Colosseum, in 'Childe Harold's Pilgrimage, Canto the Fourth' (1818)*

¶874

I walked around the old Madison Square Garden, which, so unlike the American building, embodied, in its grimness and grandeur, a human attitude that made it an official mask.

Edmund Wilson *on the Colosseum, in 'Europe without Baedeker' (1947)*

¶875

When's it going to be finished?

Spike Milligan *on the Colosseum*

¶876

Every place I look at I work out the cubic feet, and I say it will make a good warehouse or it won't. Can't help myself. One of the best warehouses I ever saw was the Vatican in Rome.

Arnold Wesker *on the Vatican, Rome*

¶877

As a whole St Peter's is fit for nothing but a ballroom, and it's a little too gaudy even for that.

John Ruskin *on the Vatican City, in a letter to the Reverend Thomas Dale (31 December 1840)*

¶878

That is a grand and solemn place, the gigantic arms inviting the concourse of all the children of men; but it is an impious work — architecture, swagger, human prowess, human greatness . . . The face of Christ has been more defiled by our praise than by spittle — for we have not praised him but ourselves.

Eric Gill *on the Vatican City, in 'Autobiography' (1940)*

¶879

On visiting Venice for the first time Robert Benchley sent a cable to Harold Ross, the editor of *The New Yorker*, reading, 'Wonderful city. Streets full of water. Please advise.'

Robert Benchley

¶880

Venice is like eating an entire box of chocolate liqueurs in one go.

Truman Capote *(26 November 1961)*

¶881

Once did she hold the gorgeous east in fee;
And was the safeguard of the west:
the worth of Venice did not fall below her birth,
Venice, the eldest child of Liberty.
She was a maiden city, bright and free;
No guile seduced, no force could violate;
And, when she took into herself a mate,
She must espouse the everlasting sea . . .
Men are we, and must grieve when even the shade
Of that which once was great is passed away.

William Wordsworth *on the extinction of the Venetian Republic*

¶882

It looks, at a distance, like a great town half floated by a deluge.

Joseph Addison *on eighteenth-century Venice, in 'Remarks on Several Parts of Italy, in the years 1701, 1702 and 1703' (1705)*

¶883

This incomparable mansion is the only paragon of all the cities in the world.

William Lithgow *on Venice, in 'Rare Adventures and Painful Peregrinations' (1614/32)*

¶884

A city for beavers.

Ralph Waldo Emerson *on Venice, in 'Journal' (June 1833)*

¶885

But close about the quays and churches, palaces and prisons: sucking at their walls, and welling up into the secret places of the town: crept the water always. Noiseless and watchful: coiled round and round it, in its many folds, like an old serpent: waiting for the time, I thought, when people should look down into its depths for any stone of the old city that had claimed to be its mistress.

Charles Dickens *on Venice, in 'Pictures from Italy' (1846)*

¶886

Who wants a Renaissance Disneyland, anyway, with entrance fees only the very rich can afford?

Private Eye *on Venice (27 October 1978)*

¶887

Tyre, the crowning city, whose merchants are princes.

Isaiah 23:8

¶888

A different place, a place which must be known to be understood and understood to be enjoyed.

Professor Quentin Hughes *on Malta*

¶889

Amsterdam did not answer our expectations; it is a kind of paltry, rubbishy Venice.

William Hazlitt *on Amsterdam, in 'Notes of a Journey through France and Italy' (1826)*

¶890

Oudna (N. Africa) was a must for suicides, a barren plain bisected by a Roman Aqueduct . . . We arrived in a great cloud of dust which improved the place.

Spike Milligan

¶891

Q: Why do you get the best view of Warsaw from the Palace of Culture?
A: Because from there you can't see the Palace of Culture.

Polish Folklore

¶892

Silently as a dream the fabric rose;
No sound of hammer or of saw was there.

William Cowper *'The Task' Bk 5 l 144. Cowper is describing the ice palace made for Catherine of Russia.*

¶893

Everything is on a vast and colossal scale, resembling that of the empire itself. The public buildings, churches, monasteries, and private palaces of the nobility, are of an immense size, and seem as if designed for creatures of a superior height and dimensions to man.

Sir N W Wraxall *on Leningrad/St Petersburg, in 'A Tour Round the Baltic' (1775)*

¶894

One does not often see a whole city being built at one moment, but this is what is happening here.

Arnold Toynbee *on Riyadh, Saudi Arabia, in 'East to West' (1958)*

¶895

The city on the Reef looked luridly beautiful in the setting sun. El Greco's Toledo, with a whiff of brimstone.

Conor Cruise O'Brien *on Johannesburg, South Africa, 'Metamorphoses of Apartheid', in 'The Observer' (22 July 1979)*

¶896

I went to have a look at the cathedral — a modern cathedral, and one of the most hideous buildings in the world. It has four crenellated spires exactly the shape of hock bottles. Unlike most of the churches in Barcelona it was not damaged during the revolution — it was spared because of its 'artistic value' people said. I think the Anarchists showed bad taste in not blowing it up when they had the chance, though they did hang a red and black banner between its spires.

George Orwell *on Barcelona Cathedral, Gaudí's Sagrada Familia, in 'Homage to Catalonia' (1938 of December 1936)*

¶897

This is the Costa del Sol, variously known as the Coca Cola Coast and the Costa Mierda, for which a genteel translation would be the Coast of Dung.

Kenneth Tynan *on the Costa del Sol, 'The Rising Costa del Sol' (1963) in 'Tynan Right and Left' (1967)*

¶898

America has few great cathedrals, but you should see some of our motels.

Herbert V Prochnow

¶899

Our national flower is the concrete cloverleaf.

Lewis Mumford

¶900

I was thinking this morning that the United States Republic has substituted an aristocracy of commercial cleverness for the old forms of aristocracy. It is said that every man has an equal chance in the US, and he has. But commercial aptitude, with as little honesty as possible, is the only thing that will be of use to him. And everything is so arranged that the 'risen' can trample on those who have not risen.

Arnold Bennett *on America, in 'Journal' (5 November 1904)*

¶901

Have you ever compared the skyline of New York or any great American city with that of a Pueblo like Taos? And did you see how the houses pile up to towers towards the centre? Without conscious imitation the American unconsciously fills out the spectral outline of the Red Man's mind and temperament.

C G Jung *'The Complications of American Psychology' (1950)*

¶902

The American sign of civic progress is to tear down the familiar and erect the monstrous.

Shane Leslie *'American Wonderland' (1936)*

¶903

The most characteristic thing in America, mechanical America, is that it can make poetry out of material things. America's poetry is not in literature, but in architecture.

Oliver St John Gogarty *'As I Was Going Down Sackville Street' (1937)*

¶904

American cities are like badger holes ringed with trash.

John Steinbeck *'Travels with Charley' (1962)*

¶905

Could that last American frontier be an amusement park?

Nicholas von Hoffman *'Spectator' (23 September 1978)*

¶906

I heard it said that the 'architecture' of Atlanta is rococola.

John Gunter *on Atlanta, in 'Inside USA' (1947)*

¶907

A snobbish Bostonian approached Whistler at a party one evening. 'And where were you born, Mr. Whistler?' she asked. 'Lowell, Massachusetts,' replied the painter. 'Whatever possessed you to be born in a place like that?' exclaimed the lady. 'The explanation is quite simple,' said Whistler. 'I wished to be near my mother.'

James Abbott McNeill Whistler

¶908

So leap with joy, be blithe and gay,
Or weep, my friends, with sorrow,
What California is today,
The rest will be tomorrow.

Richard Armour

¶909

Where was the architecture of the great city — the 'Eternal City of the West'?
Where was it? Hiding behind these shameless signs? A vacant block would come
by. Then enormous billboards planted there stood up grandly, had it all their own
way, obliterating everything in nothing. That was better. Chicago! Immense
gridiron of dirty, noisy streets . . . Heavy traffic crossing both ways at once,
managing somehow; torrential noise.

A stupid thing, that gridiron: conflicting currents of horses, trucks, street cars
grinding on hard rails, mingling with streams of human beings in seeming
confusion. Clamor! But habit was in the movement making it expert and so safe
enough. Dreary — dim — smoked. Smoked dim and smoking. A wide, desolate,
vacant strip ran along the waterfront over which the Illinois Central trains puffed,
shrieked, and ground incessantly, cutting the city off from the lake.
Terrible! This grinding and piling up of blind forces. If there was logic here, who
could grasp it?

To stop and think in the midst of this would be to give way to terror. The grey,
soiled river, with its mist of steam and smoke, was the only beauty. And that
smelled to heaven.

Frank Lloyd Wright on Chicago, in 'An Autobiography' (1979 of 1887)

¶910

Got talking to man about my travels; mentioned Parthenon by moonlight. 'Yes,'
he said, 'it may be all right, but guess it's not so big as our Masonic Temple.'

John Foster Fraser on Chicago, in 'Round the World on a Wheel' (1899)

¶911

I say God's Chicago, for who else will own it, complete it, and gather it to be the
perfect city upon earth? Chicago has all the possibilities of becoming the earth's
final city, the Babylon of the plains.

Shane Leslie on Chicago, in 'American Wonderland' (1936)

¶912

Chicago does not give itself airs and there is nothing dainty or flimsy about it,
nothing nouvelle cuisine or pretentious about its food, its people, architecture,
writing, business or politics. 'Here is a tall bold slugger set vivid against the little
soft cities', wrote Carl Sandburg in his hymn to it. It is in all ways a big-boned
and burly city and its muscular buildings stand in massive majesty like a row of
wrestlers.

It has three of the world's five tallest buildings, including the tallest, 1,450 ft,
as befits the city that gave birth to the skyscraper.

'Yes,' a radio talk show host assured a caller, 'the Sears Tower is the tallest
building in the world.' 'All right,' said the caller patiently, 'but is it the tallest
building in Chicago?'

Trevor Fishlock 'The State of America' (1986)

¶913

Chicago has a strange metaphysical elegance of death about it.

Claes Oldenburg

¶914
Here is the difference between Dante, Milton and me. They wrote about hell and never saw the place. I wrote about Chicago after looking the place over for years and years.

Carl Sandburg *quoted by Harry Golden in 'Carl Sandburg'*

¶915
Hog – Butcher for the World,
Tool Maker, stacker of Wheat,
Player with Railroads and the Nation's Freight Handler;
Stormy, husky, brawling,
City of the Big Shoulders.

Carl Sandburg *on Chicago*

¶916
O great city of visions, waging the war of the free,
Beautiful, strong and alert a goddess in purpose and mien.

Wallace Rice *on Chicago*

¶917
Pentonville is joyous to Chicago, Manchester is paradise to it,
Wapping, Whitechapel and Deptford are gardens to it.

John Masefield *in a letter to his wife, Constance (1916)*

¶918
Sputter, City! Bead with fire
Every ragged roof and spine; . . .
Burst to bloom, you proud, white flower,
But – remember that hot hour
When the shadow of your brand
Laps the last cool grain of sand –
You will still be just a scar
On a little, lonesome star.

Mildred Plew Merryman *'Chicago at Night'*

¶919
Dallas is a baby Manhattan; Fort Worth is a cattle annex.

John Gunther *on Dallas and Fort Worth, in 'Inside USA' (1947)*

¶920
Hollywood is a sewer – with service from the Ritz-Carlton.

Wilson Mizner

¶921
It's the biggest trainset a boy ever had.

Orson Welles *on Hollywood*

¶922
Strip away the phony tinsel of Hollywood and you find the real tinsel underneath.

Oscar Levant

¶923

A trip through a sewer in a glass-bottomed boat.

Wilson Mizner *on Hollywood quoted by Alva Johnson, in 'The Incredible Mizners'*
(1953) (before 1933)

¶924

California has given Art its Calvary.

Shane Leslie *on Hollywood, in 'American Wonderland' (1936)*

¶925

Hollywood, the Versailles of Los Angeles.

Jan Morris *on Hollywood, in 'Destinations' (1980)*

¶926

Las Vegas . . . is a man-made paradise, the fallen Adam in the arms of a neon
serpent. . . .This is Playland as Eden, essentially infantile, but it entrances many
bored people, including lots of foreigners.

Robert Mazzocco *on Las Vegas, 'Letter from Las Vegas', in 'New York Review of Books'*
(15 September 1977)

¶927

Long Island represents the American's idea of what God would have done with
Nature if he'd had the money.

Peter Fleming *in a letter to his brother Rupert (29 September 1929)*

¶928

. . . a city rich and vigorous and full of pride, a city lost and beaten and full of
emptiness.

Raymond Chandler *on Los Angeles*

¶929

A city seventy miles square but barely seventy years deep apart from a small
downtown not yet two centuries old and a few other pockets of ancientry, Los
Angeles is instant architecture in an instant townscape.

Professor Reyner Banham *opening lines of 'Los Angeles: The Architecture of Four*
Ecologies' (1971)

¶930

An imaginary city, Le Corbusier's Ville Radieuse, and a real one, Los Angeles,
were built as shrines to the vision of the citizen as motorist. His changed scale of
speed and distance gave rise to a city plan in which individuals were perceived as
voyagers: the neighbourhood and the street were replaced by the super-highway
and the old supportive systems in which one knew who one was by the
reflections given back by familiar faces from next door or the corner shop gave
way to the bold, curt announcement of identity made by the motor car.

Jonathan Raban *'Soft City' (1974)*

¶931

It is as though London stretched unbroken from St Albans to Southend in a tangle of ten-lane four-deck super parkways, hamburger stands, banks, topless drug-stores, hippie hide-outs, Hiltons, drive-in mortuaries, temples of obscure and extraordinary religions, sinless joy and joyless sin, restaurants built to resemble bowler hats, insurance offices built to resemble Babylon, all shrouded below the famous blanket of acrid and corroding smog.

James Cameron *on Los Angeles, in the 'Evening Standard' (9 September 1968)*

¶932

Now I know subjective opinions can vary, but personally I reckon LA as the noisiest, the smelliest, the most uncomfortable, and the most uncivilised major city in the United States. In short a stinking sewer . . .

Adam Raphael *on Los Angeles, in 'The Guardian' (22 July 1968)*

¶933

Nineteen suburbs in search of a metropolis.

H L Mencken *on Los Angeles*

¶934

The difference between Los Angeles and yoghurt is that yoghurt has real culture.

Tom Taussik *'Legless in Gaza' (1982)*

¶935

A circus without a tent.

Carey McWilliams *on Los Angeles, in 'Southern California Country' (1946)*

¶936

It was more like Egypt – the suburbs of Cairo or Alexandria – than anything in Europe. We arrived at the Bel Air Hotel – very Egyptian with a hint of Addis Ababa in the smell of the blue gums.

Evelyn Waugh *on Los Angeles, in 'Diary' (6 February 1947)*

¶937

A big hard-boiled city with no more personality than a paper cup.

Raymond Chandler *on Los Angeles, in 'The Little Sister' (1949)*

¶938

It was the first time I had seen a highway city, which was to be the model for the rest of our cities. Los Angeles is the avant-garde city of parody in architecture and even in nature (canyons and palm trees). Difficult to draw, a trap – like portraying clowns.

Saul Steinberg *'Chronology' (1950) in 'Saul Steinberg' by Harold Rosenberg (1978)*

¶939

A neighbourhood is where, when you go out of it, you get beat up.

Puerto Rican worker, *quoted in 'America Comes of Age' (1963)*

¶940

As a city, New York moves in the forefront of today's great trend of great cities towards neurosis. She is confused, self-pitying, helpless and dependent.

John Lardner *(1953)*

¶941

A sallow waiter brings me beans and pork . . .
Outside there's fury in the firmament.
Ice-cream, of course, will follow; and I'm content.
O Babylon! O Carthage! O New York!

Siegfried Sassoon *on New York, in 'Storm on Fifth Avenue'*

¶942

For minutes at a time, walking . . . through the deep canyon of down-town Broadway, I hardly felt, saw, heard or thought anything. I was a blank. The sensation of being in New York, in the midst of America's tallest buildings, with trains thundering under my feet, was so overwhelming.

Louis Adamic *'Laughing in the Jungle: The Autobiography of an Immigrant in America' (1932)*

¶943

Interviewer: How do you think Mies might regard AT & T?
Philip Johnson: I think he would be absolutely horrified.

Philip Johnson *on the AT & T Building, New York*

¶944

I am business.
I am Profit and Loss.
I am Beauty come into the Hell of the Practical.

Benjamin de Casseres *on New York, in 'Mirrors of New York' (1925)*

¶945

In New York, as once in Venice and Amsterdam, the city grows out of the water all around you, turned twice as tall by its own reflection, a perpendicular city on a horizontal sea.

Jonathan Raban *'Soft City' (1974)*

¶946

Miró breathes in the air. 'Ah, what vitamins! This city is a tonic! This city is a doctor!'

John Gruen *on Joan Miró in New York*

¶947

New York is, after all, a place of business; it is not constructed to be lived in.

Percy Wyndham Lewis *'America and Cosmic Man'*

¶948

New York is different. It is a very tight little island, not really part of the United States, it belongs to the world. It lives in an abstract world of economics and finance.

Bruce Graham *(1984)*

¶949

Where style is confused with substance, glamour mistaken for beauty and what you wear matters more than what you are.

Shirley Lowe *on New York, in a profile of the author Jay McInerney, quoted in 'The Times' (8 February 1985)*

¶950

On a visit to the United States Gorki was taken by his hosts to spend a day at Coney Island. The huge amusement park was thronged with tourists in holiday mood, and Gorki and his hosts joined in, spending the whole day sampling the sights. As they were leaving the park, they asked Gorki what he had thought of it all. After a moment's pause he said simply, 'What a sad people you must be!'

Maxim Gorki

¶951

Stone by stone we shall remove the Alhambra, the Kremlin and the Louvre and build them anew on the banks of the Hudson.

Benjamin de Casseres *on New York, in 'Mirrors of New York' (1925)*

¶952

Up in the heights of the evening skies I see my city of cities float
In sunset's golden and crimson dyes: I look and a great joy clutches my throat!
Plateau of roofs by canyons crosssed: Windows by thousands fire furled —
O gazing, how the heart is lost in the deepest city in the world.

James Oppenheim *'New York from a sky-scraper'*

¶953

We in New York celebrate the black mass of Materialism.

Benjamin de Casseres *'Mirrors of New York' (1925)*

¶954

City of hurried and sparkling waters!
City of Spires and Masts!
City nested in bays! My city!

Walt Whitman *on Manhattan*

¶955

Disneyland is for children. Manhattanland for adults.

Trevor Fishlock *'The State of America' (1986)*

¶956

Manhattan, great unfilleted sole spread out on a rock.

Le Corbusier

¶957

The only real advantage of New York is that all its inhabitants ascend to heaven right after their deaths, having served their full term in hell right on Manhattan Island.

Barnard Bulletin *(22 September 1967)*

¶958

The skyline of Manhattan changes weekly like a window display and postcards are always out of date.

Trevor Fishlock *'The State of America' (1986)*

¶959

The city of dreadful height.

James Bone *on New York, in the 'Manchester Guardian'*

¶960

Seen here in New York is the same architectural insignificance due to the national blind-spot found all the way from coast to coast except bigger and better insignificance. The insignificance we had seen all along the line had some rights. None here. Here in the greatest metropolis of the USA, in ambitious, but fatal variety, is the same deadly monotony where the building is concerned. Man-eating skyscrapers, all tall, but seeking false monumental mass for 1929 riveted steel skeletons, nineteenth century architecture. Not twentieth. The utter contradiction of structure and idea is what is most distinctive everywhere in New York.

Frank Lloyd Wright *on New York, in 'An Autobiography' (1979) (of 1929)*

¶961

At night . . . the streets become rhythmical perspectives of glowing dotted lines, reflections hung upon them in the streets as the wisteria hangs its violet racemes on its trellis. The buildings are a shimmering verticality, a gossamer veil, a festive scene-drop hanging there against the black sky to dazzle, entertain, amaze.

Frank Lloyd Wright *on New York, in 'The Disappearing City' (1932)*

¶962

'We certainly do lead the world in architecture,' said Professor Timson.
'Architecture, I take it, is the natural artistic expression of a young nation. Youth
wants to build and Manhatten Island kind of looks as though we've done what
we wanted' . . .

But what kind of youth could build like this? Some Titan's brood, or the
nurselings of Brobdingnag. Was blind Polyphemus sent to stud, and did he cover
Irish giantesses? Else how came this race that built forty storeys high to show it
had done with teething?

Eric Linklater *on New York, in 'Juan in America' (1931)*

¶963

A harlot amongst cities.

Bourke Cockran *on New York, quoted in 'American Wonderland' (1936) (of 1934) by*
Shane Leslie

¶964

New York . . . seemed to me one of the most exciting cities in the world: the
blueness of the sky floated about its pencil buildings, and shops, taxis, all human
affairs seemed to go in deep canyon-beds of natural erosion rather than among
the excrescences constructed by men. It is the only town where one's looks are
drawn all the time away from the ground into the sky: the huge buildings are not
too close together; they keep their individuality like the towers of San Gimignano
or Bologna, and from the shadow of the streets you look to their sunlight and the
long vistas of the avenues, and would not be surprised to see clouds trailing
about their summits.

Freya Stark *on New York, in 'Dust in the Lion's Paw' (1961) (of 1943)*

¶965

It is a city designed for pickpockets, the most romantic aspects of the city being
on the summits of towering buildings where the architects burst into
reminiscences of Ur of the Chaldees, the Hanging Gardens of Babylon, the
campaniles, domes and porticos of Italy and here and there the patios of Spain,
the mosques and minarets of the East. So that one is ever looking upwards from
the geometrical plan of traffic-filled avenues to a sky filled with fantasy.

Cecil Roberts *on New York, in 'And So to America' (1946)*

¶966

This rocky island, this concrete Capri.

Cyril Connolly *on New York, 'American Injection' (1947), in 'Ideas and Places' (1953)*

¶967

If one need never descend below the fortieth floor, New York would seem the
most beautiful city in the world, its skies and cloudscapes are tremendous, its
southern latitude is revealed only in its light (for vegetation and architecture are
strictly northern); here one can take in the Hudson, the East river, the mid-town
and down-town colonies of skyscrapers, Central Park and the magnificent new
bridges and curving arterial highways and here watch the evening miracle, the

lights going on all over these frowning termitaries against a sky of royal-blue velvet only to be paralleled in Lisbon or Palermo. A southern city with a southern pollution of life, yet with a northern winter imposing a control; the whole nordic energy and sanity of living crisply enforcing its authority for three of the four seasons on the violent airy babel of tongues and races; this tension gives New York its unique concentration and makes it the supreme metropolis of the present.

> **Cyril Connolly** *'American Injection' (1947), in 'Ideas and Places' (1953)*

¶968
A hundred times I have thought, New York is a catastrophe, and fifty times: it is a beautiful catastrophe.

> **Le Corbusier** *on New York, 'The Fairy Catastrophe', in 'When the Cathedrals were White' (1947)*

¶969
From the moment a New Yorker is confronted with almost any large city of Europe, it is impossible for him to pretend to himself that his own city is anything other than an unscrupulous real-estate speculation.

> **Edmund Wilson** *'Europe without Baedeker' (1947)*

¶970
A haven as cosy as toast, cool as an icebox and safe as skyscrapers.

> **Dylan Thomas** *(1950) on New York, quoted in 'Dylan Thomas in America' (1956) by J M Brinnin*

¶971
But the classic view of the New York skyline — this time the downtown skyline of Wall Street — is from the Brooklyn waterfront. Here, on my third evening in New York, I look across the river . . . to see range upon range of towers, racing upwards to a chaotic variety of heights, yet so compressed as to make an orderly form out of the chaos. I was reminded of the serried church-towers of San Gimignano, multiplied and blown up to a colossal scale — and indeed I have since noticed that San Gimignano provides a favourite subject for American painters in Italy. But these were not church-towers. They were towers filled with men. And to what purpose? Was New York, perhaps, the City of Dreamless Spires?

> **Lord Kinross** *'The Innocents at Home' (1959)*

¶972
That sinister Stonehenge of economic man, the Rockefeller Center.

> **Cyril Connolly** *'American Injection' (1947), in 'Ideas and Places' (1953)*

¶973

Images of confinement certainly haunt me in Manhattan, but the first thing that always strikes me, when I land once more on the island, is its fearful and mysterious beauty. Other cities have built higher now, or sprawl more boisterously over their landscapes, but there is still nothing like the looming thicket of the Manhattan skyscrapers, jumbled and overbearing. Le Corbusier hated this ill-disciplined spectacle, and conceived his own Radiant City, an antiseptic hybrid of art and ideology, in direct antithesis to it. His ideas, though, mostly bounced off this vast mass of vanity. Tempered though it has been from time to time by zoning law and social trend, Manhattan remains a mammoth mess, a stupendous clashing of light and dark and illusory perspective, splotched here and there by wastelands of slum or demolition, wanly patterned by the grid of its street system, but essentially, whatever the improvers do to it, whatever economy decrees or architectural fashion advises, the supreme monument to that elemental human instinct, Free-For-All.

Jan Morris *'The Islanders' Manhattan 1979, in 'Among the Cities' (1985)*

¶974

When you get there, there isn't any there there.

Gertrude Stein *on Oakland, USA*

¶975

I went to Philadelphia one Sunday. The place was closed.

W C Fields

¶976

Destroy it and start again.

Frank Lloyd Wright *on how to improve Pittsburgh*

¶977

The genius of architecture seems to have shed its maledictions over this land.

Thomas Jefferson *'Notes on the State of Virginia' (1784-85)*

¶978

As you get to know Europe, slowly tasting the wines, cheeses and characters from the different countries, you begin to realise that the important determinant of a culture is, after all, the spirit of the place.

Lawrence Durrell

¶979

There are also a lot of nice buildings in Haiphong. What their contributions are to the war effort I don't know, but the desire to bomb a virgin building is terrific.

Commander Henry Urban Jnr *on the Vietnam War*

Home Sweet Home

¶980
An Englishman's home is his castle.
Proverb

¶981
The house of every one is to him as his castle and fortress.
Sir Edward Coke

¶982
[A man's house is] the theatre of his hospitality, the seat of his self-fruition and the comfortablest part of his own life.
Sir Henry Wotton *'Elements of Architecture' (1624)*

¶983
I want a house that has got over all its troubles; I don't want to spend the rest of my life bringing up a young and inexperienced house.
Jerome K Jerome *'They and I'*

¶984
Everybody hates house-agents because they have everybody at a disadvantage. All other callings have a certain amount of give and take; the house-agent simply takes.
H G Wells

¶985

He advised that the privy should in every house be the room nearest to Heaven.
  Aldous Huxley

¶986

We should learn from the snail: it has devised a home that is both exquisite and functional.
  Frank Lloyd Wright *quoted in the 'Guardian' (1956)*

¶987

Only you can hear the houses sleeping in the streets in the slow deep salt and silent black, bandaged night. Only you can see, in the blinded bedrooms, the combinations and petticoats over the chairs, the jugs and basins, the glasses of teeth, Thou Shalt Not on the wall, and the yellowing dickybird-watching pictures of the dead. Only you can hear and see, behind the eyes of the sleepers, the movements and countries and mazes and colours and dismays and rainbows and tunes and wishes and flight and fall and despairs and big seas of their dreams.
  Dylan Thomas *'Under Milk Wood'*

¶988

I have a vision of the Future, chum:
The workers' flats, in fields of soya beans
Towering up like silver pencils, score on score,
While Surging Millions hear the Challenge come
From loudspeakers in communal canteens;
'No Right! No Wrong! All's perfect, evermore'.
  Sir John Betjeman *sending up the Brave New World of the Welfare State*

¶989

The house . . . a machine for living.
  Le Corbusier *quoted in 'The Times' (1965)*

¶990

Build the houses for the people . . . every humble home will bless you if you succeed.
  Sir Winston Churchill *to Harold Macmillan, after the Tory Party Conference in 1951 had demanded the building of 300,000 houses a year.*

¶991

It is only in a society where we have a government working day and night on our behalf that the housing problems are insoluble.
  Lord Goodman *Chairman of the Housing Corporation, addressing town planners (1973)*

¶992

Keep your home clean and tidy. Endeavour to have some method of cleaning as you go along; do not try to clean the whole house in one day. Regular bed times for children and adults, except on special occasions. Sit down properly at the table. Hang up your pots and pans or put them on a shelf . . .
  Council handbook *issued to tenants in the 1950s*

¶993

The surroundings householders crave are glorified autobiographies ghost-written by willing architects and interior designers who, like their clients, want to show off.

T H Robsjohn-Gibbings 'Robsjohn-Gibbings Names the Biggest Bore', in 'Town & Country' (January 1961)

¶994

A man's house is his stage. Others walk on to play their bit parts. Now and again a soliloquy, a birth, an adultery.

Karl Shapiro 'The Bourgeois Poet' (1964)

¶995

The house looms large, if not as a refuge, as a metaphor, live, dead and mixed. It is the repository of our wishes and dreams, memories and illusions. It is, or at least ought to be, instrumental in the transition from being to well-being.

Bernard Rudofsky 'The Prodigious Builders' (1977)

¶996

The danger about plans for housing is that, as its term of office ends, the present government will make gestures like the release of funds to local authorities and to the Housing Corporation in response to growing anxiety and anger over the lack of investment in housing, and that this will result in a crash programme to reassure the electors. In such programmes, the same assumptions about councils as direct providers of homes will be made, as though there was nothing to learn from the disasters of the past. Similarly the opposition will promise another version of the same plan. When we build again, we need not a plan for housing, but an attitude that will enable millions of people to make their own plans.

Colin Ward 'When We Build Again – Let's have housing that works!' (1985)

¶997

Our vast housing problems machine has committed one blunder after another in the name of social betterment. The betterment is often hard to find, especially if compared with what might have been, but the malaise and misery and tragedy are writ large as soon as one opens one's eyes to the facts. The brave new Utopia is essentially a device for treating people like children, first by denying them the right to choose their own kind of housing, and then by choosing for them disastrous designs that create a needless sense of social failure . . . Housing choice and responsibility for one's home should be decisions made not by the bureaucrats but by the occupants. The future should be in their own hands.

Alice Coleman 'Utopia on Trial: Vision and Reality in Planned Housing' (1985)

¶998

If I had to say which was telling the truth about society, a speech by the Minister of Housing, or the actual buildings put up in his time, I should believe the buildings.

Lord Kenneth Clark 'Civilisation' (1969)

¶999

When dwellers control the major decisions and are free to make their own contribution to the design, construction or management of their housing, both the process and the environment produced stimulate individual and social well-being. When people have no control over, nor responsibility for key decisions in the housing process, on the other hand, dwelling environments may instead become a barrier to personal fulfilment and a burden on the economy.

John Turner and Robert Fichter *'Freedom to Build' (1972)*

¶1000

Tenants of the world unite, you have nothing left to lose but your chain link fencing.

Louis Hellman *after Karl Marx*

¶1001

The best thing that ever happened to British architecture was the collapse of Ronan Point.

Theo Crosby *'How to Play the Environment Game' (1973)*

Credits

Publisher and Editor wish to thank authors, their agents, and publishers for permission to reprint copyright material in this anthology. Every effort has been made to trace the copyright holder for each quotation, and to make full acknowledgement for its use. If errors or omissions have occurred inadvertently, they will be corrected or rectified in subsequent editions provided notification is sent to the publisher. References are to the numbered quotations.

Academy Editions, London: 92, 648 reproduced from, Terry Farrell *Architectural Monograph* 1984, Academy Editions, London, 649 reproduced from Terry Farrell *Architectural Monograph* 1984, Academy Editions, London

Allen & Unwin (Publishers) Ltd: 402

Amereon House: 940 from *Strong Cigars & Lonely Women*

The Architectural Press: 23 © Museum of Modern Art, New York; 275

Argyll Songs Ltd: 650

Associated Book Publishers (UK) Ltd: 109 published by Methuen (1980), 901 published by Routledge and Kegan Paul (1950)

BBC Publications: 579

Marion Boyars: 440

Extracts from *Pass the Port Again* published by Christian Brann Limited, Phoenix Way, Cirencester, Glos: 113, 176, 686, 810

Butterworth & Co (Publishers) Ltd: 339

Cambridge University Press: 123, 645

Campbell, Thomson, McLaughlin: 328

Jonathan Cape Limited: 80, 289 Tom Wolfe, 376, 499, 605, 606

Century Hutchinson Limited (1986): page 10 from *Ghastly Good Taste* by Sir John Betjeman

Rosalind Cole (Literary Agents): 286 © Andy Warhol

Collins Publishers (Fontana Books): 560, 809, 930, 945

Reprinted from Bartlett's *Unfamiliar Quotations* © 1971 by Leonard Louis Levinson, used with permission of Contemporary Books, Inc. Chicago: 417, 790, 799

© Theo Crosby: 167, 272, 423, 1001 (all published by Arts Council and Penguin Books)

Edward Cullinan, architect: 212 © Edward Cullinan, RIBA Publications

The Devin-Adair Co Inc: 86 © Selden Rodman

Andre Deutsch Ltd: 257, 288 (1976), 502, 721, 835 from *Contemporary Guide to Economics, Peace and Laughter* (1971), 938

Reprinted by permission of Doubleday & Company, Inc: 146, 150, 173 from *Streets for People* by Bernard Rudofsky copyright © 1964, 1969 by Bernard Rudofsky

Duckworth Publishers: 380, 691

Giulio Einaudi Editore: page 9 from *Theories and History of Architecture* by Manfredo Tafuri

Lord Esher: 631

Reprinted by permission of Faber and Faber: 372 from *The Dyer's Hand*, Auden, 415 *Look back in anger*, 490 *Collected Poems* by W H Auden, 532 from *A Certain World* by W H Auden, 576 from *Choruses from 'The Rock': Collected Poems 1909–1962* by T S Eliot, 578 from 'Going Going' *High Windows* by Philip Larkin, 615 from 'Marginalia' *Collected Poems* by W H Auden, 624 from *The Entertainer*, 742 from 'The Fire Sermon'

The Waste Land, 751 from *The Waste Land*, 978 from *Spirit of Place – Letters and Essays on Travel* (1969) Lawrence Durrell

The Frontier Press Co: 908 (Hammond 1957)

With kind permission from Walter Shewring, literary executor of Eric Gill: 684 © Eric Gill, 878 © Eric Gill

Glidrose Publications: 805

Victor Gollancz Ltd: 427

Gower Publishing Company Limited: 634, 658

Grafton Books, A Division of the Collins Publishing Group: 824

Grasset et Fasquelle Editions, Paris: 201

Greater London Council (London Residuary Board): 651

Greenwood Press, Inc. Westport, CT: 378, 902, 911, 924

Jane Gregory: 996 Pluto Press 1985

Hamish Hamilton: 906, 919, 937

Harcourt, Brace & World: 400 (1963)

Harper & Row Publishers Inc: 994

Harvard University Press: 573

A M Heath & Company Limited, Authors' Agents: 896 The estate of the late Sonia Brownell Orwell and Secker & Warburg Ltd

Reprinted by permission of William Heinemann Limited: 83, 904 *Travels with Charley: In Search of America* (1962)

David Higham Associates Limited: 735 © Elisabeth Lutyens, 987 from *Under Milk Wood* published by J M Dent & Sons

Reprinted by permission of Hodder & Stoughton Limited: 533 from *Betjeman Country* by Frank Delaney

The Hogarth Press: 848, 849, 874, 969

Michael Imison Playwrights Ltd: 249, 438

Jameson Books, Ottawa, IL: 619

Michael Joseph Ltd: 491, 621

Kennikat Press: 842

Alfred A Knopf, Inc: 25 *Themes and Episodes* by Igor Stravinsky and Robert Craft (1966)

Longman Group Publishers: 879 from *Tynan Right and Left: Plays, Films, People, Places and Events* (1967)

© Owen Luder: 327

Lund Humphries Publishers: 382 *Fortress: Architecture and Military History in Malta* by Quentin Hughes (1969)

Macdonald & Co (Publishers) Ltd: 939 from *America Comes of Age: The Era of Theodore Roosevelt* (1971)

McClelland and Steward Ltd, Toronto: 397

McGraw-Hill Book Company (Publishers): 520, 521

Millington Press: 478

The MIT Press: 255 *Collage City* (1978) by Colin Rowe and Fred Koetter, 472 from *The Definitive Edition of the Works of George Santayana*. Edited by H J Saatkamp Jr and William G (1944)

Muller, Blond & White Ltd: 153

John Murray (Publishers) Ltd: 408, 419, 420 *Cartoon History of Architecture*, 421 617 *The Castles on the Ground: The Anatomy of Suburbia*, 677 *Collected Poems*, 685 from *Oxford Dictionary of Quotations*, 749 *Collected Poems*, 787 *Collected Poems*, 912, 955, 964 *Dust in the Lion's Paw: Autobiography 1939–46* (1961), 971, 988 *The Planster's Vision* from *Collected Poems*, 998 (BBC & John Murray)

The Nonesuch Press: 414 (1948)

Index of Sources

References given in the index relate to numbered quotations, not pages.

Index of Themes

References given in the index relate
to numbered quotations, not pages.